church
next

using the internet
to maximize
your ministry

church
next

aubrey malphurs
michael malphurs

Kregel
Academic & Professional

Church Next: Using the Internet to Maximize Your Ministry

Published by Kregel Publications, a division of Kregel, Inc., P.O. Box 2607, Grand Rapids, MI 49501.

Library of Congress Cataloging-in-Publication Data
Malphurs, Aubrey.
Church next: using the internet to maximize your ministry / by Aubrey Malphurs and Michael Malphurs.
     p. cm.
Includes bibliographical references and index.
    1. Internet in church work—United States. 2. Internet—Religious aspects—Christianity. I. Malphurs, Michael. II. Title.
BV652.77.M35   2003
261.5'2'090511—dc21   2003012161

ISBN 0-8254-3185-9

Printed in the United States of America

03 04 05 06 07 / 5 4 3 2 1

Contents

Introduction

It's quiet at 1:00 A.M. All that can be heard is the clicking of keys as twenty-five-year-old Andrew, a relatively new Christian, types on his laptop. He's been online for the past half hour, sharing his faith with a guy who identifies himself only as Mark. Mark has many questions about the faith, and Andrew, with an open Bible in front of him, types and clicks about God's love and grace in sending Christ to die for his sins.

Mary, an elderly lady whose arthritic condition has confined her to a wheelchair in a nursing home, is not able to get out much anymore. What she misses most is attending church every Sunday. Although it was difficult at first, she has learned to use a computer enough to be a part of her church's prayer team—actually, she's become the team leader. Her visitors often comment that they can hear the clicking of keys down the hall as they approach her room. And the word around church is that if you have an urgent prayer need, e-mail it to Mary Smith, who's affectionately known as the "prayer lady."

Although Susan has never been outside the United States, she's heavily involved in her church's missions ministry. Last year, her small church of approximately seventy-five people took a bold step and went online with a Web site. Next, they added evangelistic Web pages and a chat room, hoping to reach some of the unchurched in their community. Much to their surprise, people from different countries, including China and a number of predominantly Muslim countries, contacted the church through its site. They were curious about Christianity and simply wanted to know more. Susan, who has been a

Christian since childhood, is quick to confess that she has never been one to share her faith and once had little interest in missions. Now, with her newfound passion, she devotes two evenings a week to respond to the numerous requests from internationals for more information about Christianity.

A question that many people are asking these days is what the church of the twenty-first century will look like. Regardless of the ultimate answer, it seems clear that Andrew, Mary, and Susan are part of a new era for the church. One thing they have in common is their use of the Internet for ministry. Perhaps the most profound technological advance since Johannes Gutenberg's invention of the printing press, the Internet presents the church with the potential—more than at any other time—to pursue the Great Commission and reach the entire world for the Savior.

Researcher George Barna, director of the Barna Institute, predicts that by 2010 as many as fifty million people may rely on the Internet to provide their faith-based experiences. Although Americans are just beginning to warm to the concept of cyberfaith, he says, as this decade advances, as many as two-thirds, especially teenagers, will engage in Net-based religious pursuits such as listening to religious teaching, reading online devotionals, and purchasing religious products.

Some people are already moving in that direction. In a recent interview with Korean pastor David Yonggi Cho, Rick Warren of Saddleback Valley Community Church said, "We wanted to prove to the world that you don't have to have a building to grow a church. We were running over ten thousand in attendance before we built our first building. So we know how to grow and minister without buildings. But what we are trying to learn now is how to do it through Internet into the homes."

"It's exactly the Internet service!" Cho added. "It is silly to build larger and larger church buildings. It is silly to spend more money on (branch church) buildings! You'll never have enough. I really believe this, and I have already announced to my people and ministers that the next step is to go into total cyberspace ministry because it is a real waste of money to build larger buildings."[1]

Some will no doubt argue that churches shouldn't use the Internet—because it's a medium for pornography, it encourages reclusive behavior, or it's too expensive. However, these arguments could also have been used against the printing press, the telephone, the fax machine, e-mail, and other means of communication technology. Our position is that the Internet is simply a tool that one can use for or against the cause of Christ. The tool itself is not the problem but how the tool is used.

Initially, such technology may frighten some churches. However, it's not difficult to predict what forward-thinking, Christ-honoring churches will do with the Internet. Like the printing press, the Internet will continue to exert a huge influence on the culture of the twenty-first century and on the rapidly increasing number of people who use it daily. The question facing the church is what it will do with this technology. The chapters that follow will explore how leading-edge churches are using the Internet and how the church at large could use this technology in the future.

We've divided our discussion into three parts: problem, solution, and method. In part 1, we explore the problem of the decline of American Christianity. In part 2, we suggest a solution to the problem: reaching a new generation and an older generation for Christ. In part 3, we articulate a primary method for reaching the generations through eMinistry.

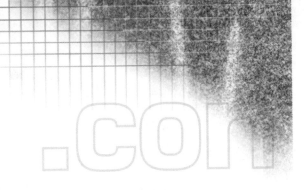

part one

The Problem:
American Christianity
Is in Decline

chapter one

The State of the Church

The church is God's ordained means for reaching the world—or, as Bill Hybels has said, the church is the hope of the world. Jesus said, "I will build my church, and the gates of Hades will not overcome it" (Matt. 16:18). In Matthew 28:19–20, Jesus reveals how he will use the church to reach the world when He says to the eleven disciples, "Therefore go and make disciples of all nations." We know that Jesus wasn't speaking exclusively to the eleven disciples because in Acts 1:8 he expands their vision for sharing the gospel to include "the ends of the earth"—which became the mission of the church.

Every January, the president of the United States gives a State of the Union address. It naturally follows the president's inaugural address, which casts his vision for the future of the nation. The State of the Union message is designed to answer the question of how we are progressing as a nation. Although highly politicized, it's an annual update on how well the president is accomplishing his inaugural vision.

The American church would be wise to follow the president's example and examine the state of American Christianity each year. How are we are doing in reaching our neighbors for Christ? How is Christianity progressing in America?

In order to answer these questions, we must look at the state of the church in North America. If the church is the hope of the world, the question of how Christianity is doing becomes, How is *the church* doing? The answer to this important spiritual question is that, in the early twenty-first century, the church isn't doing well. American Christianity is in decline. Our purpose in this chapter is to present three reasons for this decline,

Churches Have Plateaued and Are Declining

All organizations pass through a life cycle that consists of the following phases: birth, growth, plateau, decline, and death (fig. 1). The church is not immune to this life cycle. If you were to visit Israel and Asia Minor today, you would not find any of the first-century churches mentioned in the New Testament. They all passed through the cycle and are gone, yet the church as an organization still exists because those early churches gave birth to successive generations of churches.

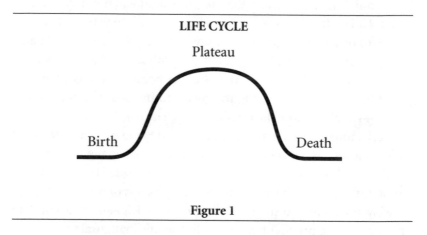

LIFE CYCLE

Plateau

Birth

Death

Figure 1

Win Arn, a church-growth researcher, contrasts the state of the church at the end of the twentieth century with the church in the 1950s: "In the years following World War II, thousands of new churches were established. Today, of the approximately 350,000 churches in America, four out of five are either plateaued or declining."[1] In other words, Arn's research reveals that 80 to 85 percent of the churches in America are on the downside of the growth cycle.[2]

In one of the most comprehensive surveys ever conducted on American faith communities, Carl Dudley and David Roozen discovered that more than one-half of all congregations predate World War II, in terms of their founding.[3] Lyle Schaller observes that "66 percent to 75 percent of all congregations founded before 1960 are either on a plateau in size or shrinking in numbers."[4]

How Are Mainline Churches Doing?

According to Benton Johnson, Dean Hoge, and Donald Luidens:

America's so-called mainline Protestant churches aren't what they used to be. For generation on end, the Methodists, Presbyterians, Congregationalists, Episcopalians, and kindred denominations reported net annual membership gains. As recently as the 1950s, their growth rate equaled or exceeded that of the United States as a whole.

But in the early 1960s their growth slowed down, and after the middle of the decade they had begun to lose members. With very few exceptions, the decline has continued to this date. Never before had any large religious body in this country lost members steadily for so many years.[5]

The United Methodist Church dropped from approximately 11 million members in 1965 to 8.3 million in 2001. In the same period, the Presbyterian Church (USA) lost one-fourth of its people, falling from 4 million to 3 million members; the Disciples of Christ dropped from 2 million to less than 1 million (losing one-half of their people); and the Episcopal Church fell from 3.4 million members to 2.3 million (approximately one-fourth).[6]

How Are Evangelical Churches Doing?

Although some theologically conservative churches are growing, the majority are not. According to data collected by the Hartford Institute for Religion Research and reported in *Faith Communities Today,* two growing conservative groups—megachurches and the Assemblies of God—reported at least a 10 percent gain in regularly participating adults from 1995 to 2000. In order to be classified as a megachurch, a congregation must have at least two thousand people in attendance. According to Hartford Seminary researcher Scott Thumma, these large congregations developed rapidly during the last two decades (1980–2000), when attendance shot up an average of 90 percent.[7] However, less than 10 percent of the churches in America are megachurches.

The Assemblies of God have also experienced rapid growth, in part because of the denomination's strong emphasis on church planting.[8] In addition, some researchers in the past have noted that growth in conservative groups has been more the result of "a kind of circulation process by which evangelicals move from one conservative church to another."[9] Two researchers concluded that "conservative churches do a better job of retaining those already familiar with evangelical culture—both transfers and children of members—than moderate and liberal churches do in retaining their members."[10]

The primary evidence for conservative church growth, according to Dean Kelley in his popular yet controversial 1972 book, *Why Conservative Churches Are Growing*, was the comparison of official church membership figures between conservative and mainline denominations.[11] Tom Smith, however, questioned this evidence, specifically the conclusion that conservative churches were growing. He cited several reasons why he believed growth had been exaggerated. For example, he believed that growth might have been found in denominations that weren't typical of all conservative churches or denominations. Also, the figures might not have been accurate because of exaggeration or unintentional overcounting by conservatives who placed greater emphasis on growth and conversion.[12]

Two conservative denominations will serve to illustrate Smith's concerns. First, the conservative Lutheran Church, Missouri Synod, declined in membership from 2,788,536 people in 1970 to 2,582,440 in 2001.[13] Second, the conservative Southern Baptist denomination, which had traditionally seen a growth in members since 1926, reported a statistical stall in 1987 in some denominational programs. When pollster George Gallup reviewed the statistics, he reported, "Southern

Baptist statistics appear to represent a leveling out rather than a reversal or sudden turnaround."[14] Then, in 1998, church membership in Southern Baptist churches registered a one-year decrease from 15,891,514 to 15,729,356 (1.02 percent). The number of Southern Baptist churches declined from 40,887 in 1997 to 40,870 in 1998 (0.04 percent), and the number of baptisms dropped from 412,027 to 407,264 (1.16 percent). However, in that same period, Sunday morning worship attendance increased by 3.33 percent.[15]

My (Aubrey) experience in traveling across America as a church consultant and working with various churches is that many of them are in serious decline. In fact, I rejoice when I hear of a church that is growing and reaching lost people, because I don't hear that good report very often. Although some denominations deny the obvious, others have turned to vigorous programs of church planting, knowing that starting new churches is the key to their survival.

The Number of Churched People Is Declining

While many mainline and conservative churches have plateaued or declined, the number of churched people in North America has also declined. This finding calls into question how many people are churched, who isn't churched, and the accuracy of the figures.

How Many People Are Churched?

One way to examine American adult church attendance is to look at the polls. In 1986, the Barna Research Group began tracking American church attendance. Table 1 presents Barna's findings from 1986 to 2001.[16]

Barna describes the picture from the mid-1980s through the mid-1990s as that of a church on a roller coaster. In 1986, 42 percent of adults attended a church service during a typical week in January. The roller coaster reached its peak of 49 percent in 1991. However, it plummeted in 1996 to its lowest point of 37 percent. It rose to 40 percent in 2000 and to 42 percent in late July to mid-August before the terrorist

attacks of September 11, 2001. In the months following the assault (late
October to early November), attendance rose to 48 percent, its highest point since 1991. However, the Barna material doesn't reflect a drop
in attendance in November 2001 that was recorded in polling by the
George Gallup organization. Nevertheless, Barna's findings show that
the average church attendance between 1986 and 2001 was 43 percent,
with a high of 49 percent and a low of 37 percent.

BARNA CHURCH ATTENDANCE TRENDS

Year	Attended in Last Week
2001	48%
(late October and	
early November)	
2001	42%
(late July and mid-August)	
2000	40%
1996	37%
1991	49%
1986	42%

Table 1

The Gallup Organization has been recording American church attendance since 1939 and currently provides the most comprehensive
research on church attendance. The Gallup pollsters ask the trend
question: Did you, yourself, happen to attend church or synagogue in
the last seven days, or not? Consequently, the results contain figures
for both church and synagogue attendance, although the latter number is slight. Although Gallup's numbers (table 2) are different from
Barna's, they reflect a similar "church on a roller coaster ride" pattern.[17]

GALLUP CHURCH ATTENDANCE TRENDS

Year	Attended in Last Week
2001	43%
2000	43%
1999	43%
1998	40%
1997	40%
1996	38%
1995	43%
1994	42%
1993	40%
1992	40%
1991	42%
1990	40%
1989	43%
1988	42%
1987	40%
1985	42%
1983	40%
1982	41%
1981	41%
1979	40%
1972	40%
1969	42%
1967	42%
1962	46%
1958	49%
1957	47%
1955	49%
1954	49%
1950	39%
1940	37%
1939	41%

Table 2

The average number of American adults who attended a church or synagogue between 1939 to the present is 42 percent. The roller coaster hit its peak between 1954 and 1962 with a high of 49 percent in 1954–55 and again in 1958. The average for this period was 48 percent. The church roller coaster hit its lowest point in 1996 at 38 percent.

Apparently, American religious attendance was up in 2001. However, the Gallup polls reflect what would have been a drop in average attendance from 43 percent to around 41 percent had the terrorist attack on the World Trade Center not taken place (table 3).[18]

GALLUP CHURCH ATTENDANCE TRENDS FOR 2001

Question: Did you, yourself, happen to attend church or synagogue in the last seven days, or not?

	Yes	No
2001 (Nov. 8–11)	42%	58%
2001 (Sept. 21–22)	47%	53%
2001 (May 10–14)	41%	59%
2001 (Feb. 19–21)	41%	59%

Table 3

Nevertheless, when compared to surveys of church attendance in Europe, the Gallup polls indicate that America is one of the more religious nations in the industrialized West, and thus might still be thought of as a Christian nation—at least sort of. In response to a 1988 Gallup survey, Thomas Reeves asked:

How can that much faith exist in a secular society? If 84 percent of its people believe that Jesus Christ was what he said he was, doesn't that by definition qualify the United States as a Christian country? Gallup concluded that "the degree of religious orthodoxy found among Americans is simply amazing. . . . Such a nation cannot by any stretch of the imagination be described as secular in its core beliefs." And Gallup's response to America's level of faith in the Christian gospel is that it's "simply amazing."[19]

How Accurate Are the Statistics?

All of this statistical information assumes the accuracy of the polls. But how accurate are they? How much should we trust self-identification or self-reporting surveys that take respondents at their word? Is America secular or Christian?

Commenting on one of his polls, Louis Harris admitted, "It should be noted that church attendance is notoriously overreported as a socially desirable activity, so true attendance figures are surely lower than those reported here."[20] Barry Kosmin is codirector of the 2001 American Religious Identification Survey (ARIS), an ongoing study conducted by the Graduate Center of the City University of New York. He notes in an article in *USA Today*, "Leadership of all faiths exaggerate or manufacture their numbers."[21]

In 1994, a team of sociologists led by C. Kirk Hadaway challenged the view that approximately 40 percent of Americans were weekly church attenders.[22] In their article titled "What the Polls Don't Show," using the same Gallup question, they found that only 20 percent of Protestants and 28 percent of Roman Catholics show up on Sundays, in contrast to Gallup's figures, which cite 45 percent of Protestants and 51 percent of Catholics. The team based its figures on actual head counts of Protestant attendance in Ashtabula County, Ohio, and of Catholics in eighteen dioceses across the country. Thus, they argued that poll respondents in self-reports overstate substantially their actual church attendance. They suggested several explanations, one of which was that people like to see or present themselves as being better than they are—what we might call a "halo effect." The same is true when people are polled about their voting or their charitable giving. The Hadaway team concluded that the actual attendance rate has declined since World War II, in spite of surveys suggesting that it has basically remained stable.

I (Aubrey) and many church pastors are not surprised at these findings. I've spent much of my life teaching at Dallas Seminary and consulting with and ministering to churches in the Dallas-Fort Worth metroplex, which is popularly viewed as "the buckle" on the Bible Belt. Even in this part of the country, where it seems there's a church on every street corner, most people would be surprised to hear that as many or more than 40 percent of the people attend church. Although we have more churches than do most places in America, many of them have plateaued or are in decline with failing attendance. In fact, one pastor cited a survey indicating that in Plano (a town just north of Dallas), 74 percent of the residents do not belong to a church.[23] Another church, in Arlington (just west of Dallas), estimates that 74 percent of the 270,000 residents of Arlington don't attend church.[24]

Another question is whether the polls reflect American population growth. At issue is whether they take into account annual increases in the American population. If the population is growing, it would mean that more people each year would need to attend church to hold steady at a 40 percent figure. In a later article titled "Did You Really Go to Church This Week?" C. Kirk Hadaway and Penny Marler believe they don't:

> If the percentage of Americans attending church is stable, aggregate church membership should have increased as the American population grew. But after adding together denominational membership statistics (including estimates of membership for independent congregations) we found that the aggregate membership total has been virtually static since the late 1960s.[25]

Hadaway and Marler responded to criticism of their research by returning to Ashtabula County, Ohio, where they had done much of their original research. Actually, the purpose of their visit was to add a Roman Catholic attendance count to their previous count of Protestants:

> We attended a total of 38 masses in 13 parishes over several months, counting attendance at each mass. Our counts

showed that 24 percent of Catholics attended mass during an average week. In a poll of Ashtabula County residents, however, 51 percent of Roman Catholic respondents said they attended church during the past week.[26]

Hadaway and his team followed a similar procedure in evaluating church attendance in Oxford County in southern Ontario, Canada. The results confirmed that a large gap also existed in church attendance in Canada. Again, they addressed the issue of why people overreported their attendance. They cited several reasons, one of which was that "most people report what they usually do, what they would like to do, or what they think someone like them *ought* to do."[27] They drew the following conclusions:

> Too much trust in survey data has produced a distorted image of religion in America by masking declines in church participation. Church attendance is less strong and stable than poll data show. Still many Americans continue to hold the church in great esteem and define themselves in traditional religious terms. The increasing gap between doing and saying reflects these countertrends.[28]

It is doubtful that this pattern of overreporting attendance will continue indefinitely, because when people stop going to church, eventually they stop feeling the need to say that they still attend. However, this conclusion is only a guess. The answer lies in the behavior of generations to come.

Who Isn't Churched?

Pollster George Barna addressed the issue of who isn't churched in a survey conducted in 1999 (table 4).[29]

CHURCH ATTENDANCE ACCORDING TO GENERATIONS	
Generation	**Percentage Attending Church**
Builders (born before 1946)	51
Boomers (born 1946–64)	41
Busters (born 1965–1976)	34
Bridgers (born 1977–1994)	29

Table 4

Unmistakably, the younger generations (Busters and Bridgers) are increasingly unchurched. Barna indicates that only 34 percent of Busters and 29 percent of Bridgers report attending church. But if these figures are *overreported*, as sociologists such as Hadaway and Marler would argue, then the real figures might be that only 17 percent of Busters and 15 percent of Bridgers actually attend church. If it's true that people who don't attend church eventually stop feeling the need to say they do, we would predict that, over time, these younger generations will report their actual attendance, and American church attendance figures will dip closer to reality. Regardless, the real concern here is over the younger generations' lack of belief and interest in Christ's church.

When asked why they didn't attend church more often, few expressed any deep animosity against the church. Only 8 percent claimed they disagreed with such things as policy and teaching. Many of them said they were either too busy or simply didn't believe that church attendance was all that important.[30]

Some Cults and Non-Christian Faiths Are Growing

A third reason why the church—and thus Christianity—is in decline in America is the growth of various cults and non-Christian faiths across the continent. The church's decline has created a spiritual vacuum that others have rushed to fill. It's both significant and alarming that several major cults have almost tripled in size and that other religious groups are prospering.

The Cults

One group that is growing *and* prospering is the Mormons. In 1992, *U.S. News and World Report* reported the following:

> Today the Church of Jesus Christ of Latter-Day Saints, better known as the Mormon Church, is one of the world's richest and fastest-growing religious movements. Since World War II, its ranks have quadrupled to more than 8.3 million members worldwide. With 4.5 million U.S. members, Mormonism already outnumbers Presbyterians and Episcopalians combined. If current trends hold, by some estimates they will number 250 million worldwide by 2080 and surpass all but the Roman Catholic Church among Christian bodies.[31]

According to the *Yearbook of American and Canadian Churches*, the Mormon Church has almost tripled from 1,789,175 in 1965 to 5,113,409 in 2001.[32] In 2002, the *Dallas Morning News* published the following report:

> For the first time, the Church of Jesus Christ of Latter-Day Saints is reported within the five largest churches in the United States, according to the National Council of Churches 2002 *Yearbook of American and Canadian Churches.*
> "This ranking represents a very brisk increase in membership for a church with a relatively brief history," said the Rev. Eileen W. Lindner, the yearbook's editor. The Latter-Day Saints were organized in 1830.[33]

The *Yearbook of American and Canadian Churches* reports that between 1988 and 2001 the Jehovah's Witnesses grew from 330,358 to 990,340.[34]

Non-Christian Faiths

An example of a non-Christian faith that has taken root and flour-ished in America is Islam. According to a study released by the Hart-ford Seminary, Muslim mosques are springing up in cities and suburbs across America.[35]

This rapid growth in the number of mosques in the last decade parallels the growth of the Mormons and the Assemblies of God. Dr. Jane I. Smith points out that in the 1980s and 1990s, generous con-tributions from abroad helped construct mosques and Islamic cen-ters. However, in the early twenty-first century, American Muslims are responsible for most of their own construction.

> According to the FACT survey, the number of mosques in the United States increased 42 percent between 1990 and 2000, compared with a 12 percent average increase among oldline Protestant, Catholic and Orthodox groups. The Latter-Day Saints and Assemblies of God congregations exceeded the evangelical average, but fell short of the growth in the num-ber of mosques.[36]

This study suggests that Islam is one of the fastest growing religious groups in the United States and that American Muslims are eager to become full and accepted participants in the mainstream of Ameri-can cultural, political, and religious life.

According to the 2001 ARIS study, the Buddhist and Hindu faiths have also experienced significant growth this past decade. From 1990 to 2001, the number of Buddhists grew 109.5 percent, and Hindus have increased at 237.4 percent. Perhaps the greatest surprise is the growth of Wicca. According to the ARIS study, the number of self-proclaimed witches has increased from 8,000 in 1990 to 134,000 in 2001—an eyebrow-raising growth of 1,575 percent.[37]

Many indicators signal that the American church is in deep trouble at the beginning of the twenty-first century. In this chapter, we've looked at three of those indicators: the plateau and decline of churches all across the country, the decline in the number of churched Americans, and the growth of cults such as Mormonism and non-Christian faiths such as Islam.

As the church goes, so goes Christianity. The question is whether the typical American church understands what is taking place and what the implications are. Perhaps Thom Rainer said it best: "America is clearly becoming less Christian, less evangelized, and less churched. Yet, too many of those in our churches seem oblivious to this reality."[38] It's time for the church and its leaders to wake up.

Questions for Reflection and Discussion

1. Before reading this chapter, were you aware of the state of the typical American church and thus Christianity in America? Do you believe that your church is aware of this situation?
2. Where would you place your church on the organizational cycle: growing, plateaued, or declining? On what do you base this assessment?
3. If your church is growing, how do you explain it?
4. If your church has plateaued or is declining, how do you explain it? What do you plan to do about your situation?

chapter two

The Buck
Stops Here!

ften, we Americans find it difficult to accept the blame for our mistakes. Instead, we follow a time-honored tradition that someone—
maybe Adam—labeled "passing the buck." We would argue that the
slumbering American church would do better to adopt the slogan
made famous by President Harry S. Truman: "The buck stops here!"

Chapter 1 identified serious problems that confront American
Christianity and the institutional American church in the early twenty-
first century. The temptation is to move quickly toward a solution
because the soul of the nation and the souls of its people are in the
balance. However, wisdom dictates that we pause and explore some
of the reasons for the decline of Christianity and the church in North
America. By identifying the reasons for our problems, we may more
easily find solutions to those problems. First, we'll look at some of the
reasons why people—those whom we're trying to reach for the Savior—aren't attending our churches. Next, we'll examine the churches
themselves—those whom Christ has commissioned to reach the lost—
to see how they might be contributing to the problem.

Why Americans Aren't Attending Church

Americans enjoy far more freedom than most other people in the
world. The First Amendment to the Constitution guarantees every
citizen freedom of religion. Unlike other countries, such as those that

embrace Islam and insist that their people hold to the Muslim faith, Americans are free to worship when and where they choose—or not worship at all. In short, they can "take it or leave it." Most Americans "vote with their feet." If they think the church is addressing their spiritual needs, they'll attend; if not, many walk away. Three primary reasons explain why some people have chosen to walk away from the church: people today think differently; their faith is no longer tied to the church; and Sunday is no longer considered sacred. Let's examine each of these three in turn.

People Think Differently

One reason that many people don't attend church frequently (or at all) is that they think differently than the typical churchgoer. As Carl Dudley and David Roozen have shown, more than half of America's congregations predate World War II.[1] Although nothing is wrong with being an older congregation, far too many churches still think and act as if they are living in the prewar period. However, in the twenty-first century, our country and the way it thinks has changed dramatically compared to the past sixty or seventy years.

How are we different? Before World War II people typically lived in a monocultural world. America was largely white, Anglo-Saxon, and Protestant or Catholic. Travel was difficult, and fewer people vacationed or conducted business overseas. Consequently, Americans were not familiar with the people of other countries or those of different religious persuasions. The typical unchurched unbeliever was a young college student who would challenge the church with the question "Is there a God?" or "Does God exist?"

That world no longer exists. People today live in a multicultural society in which CNN can transport them anyplace in the world at the click of a remote control. Young, unchurched adults are asking a different question. Today's question is, "Which God is real?" The Internet and other media sources have exposed the average American to various non-Christian faiths such as Judaism, Buddhism, Hinduism, and, most recently, Islam. Of those people who are engaged in religious activities online, 50 percent use the Internet to research other faiths.[2] Churches that are set up to answer the so-called real-life questions that people are no longer asking are set up for failure. The majority of Americans is responding to the traditional church's invitation to "come meet with us on our terms" with a polite "no thanks."

People's Faith Is No Longer Tied to the Church

Another reason that people no longer attend church is because their faith isn't inextricably tied to the church or its leadership. Early in 1990, Gallup discovered that an overwhelming number of both the churched and the unchurched believed that people "should arrive at their religious beliefs independent of any church or synagogue." Furthermore, one could be a good Christian or Jew without necessarily participating in a Christian or Jewish faith community.[3] And how important are the clergy to that faith process? Gallup found that 67 percent of the populace had confidence in the clergy in 1985, but between 1992 and 1995, that figure dropped 13 percentage points to 54 percent.[4]

Does this mean that these people are upset with or even angry at the institution of the church? Not necessarily. When asked why they no longer attend church, many unchurched people thought that the church simply wasn't that important; 34 percent said they were just too busy.[5]

As a culture, when it comes to church attendance, as with so many other aspects of life, Americans are individualists who pride themselves on their personal autonomy to do what they want to do. Wade Roof and William McKinney write, "Typically, Americans view religious congregations as gatherings of individuals who have chosen to be together, in institutions of their own making and over which they hold control—fostering what sometimes, in the eyes of observers from other countries, appears as 'churchless Christianity.'"[6]

The issue is one of authority. Who determines what we should believe and do? Far too many Americans are individualists who are convinced that "religious authority lies in the believer—not in the church, not in the Bible, despite occasional claims of infallibility and inerrancy on the part of some."[7]

Sunday Morning Is No Longer Sacred

A third reason people no longer attend church is that Sunday morning is no longer sacred. As we observed in chapter 1, the church reached its highest attendance levels between 1954 and 1962 according to Gallup's statistics. Church attendance offered respectability. Going to church was what proper, middle-class, suburban people did on Sunday mornings. Participation in church coincided with an emphasis on the family. It was also associated with patriotism, coupled with a strong belief in government and most other major institutions. During this time, American culture also became largely a churched culture in some parts of the United States, such as the South. Going to church is what many people in the South and some parts of the North did on Sunday mornings. Some cities had blue laws that prohibited stores from opening on Sundays. For some people, church was the only thing to do on Sunday mornings besides sleep in.

However, all that has changed in most of America. Sunday mornings are no longer sacred, and a number of rivals have surfaced to compete with the church for the hearts and souls of the American citizenry. One rival is the shopping mall. With the repeal of the blue laws—allowing stores to open on Sunday—some people now had to work on Sundays, and others now had someplace other than church to go.

I (Aubrey) was pastoring my second church when the blue laws were repealed in Texas in the 1980s. I wasn't in favor of the blue laws, thinking that the church could "hold its own," but I came to understand their impact on the church when one of my members told me that he wouldn't be around much on Sundays anymore because his store now was open, and he had to work to keep his job.

Another rival is sports, both participant and spectator sports. Early in the second half of the twentieth century, only professional football—and, later, basketball—competed with church for "customers" on Sunday. At the end of the twentieth century and into the twenty-first century, however, all of that has changed. On a given Sunday in December in Dallas ("the buckle on the Bible Belt"), one can attend a Dallas Cowboys football game, a Dallas Mavericks basketball game, or a Dallas Stars hockey game. If one prefers to participate actively in a sport, there's softball, touch football, and numerous soccer leagues. Other people like to jog around the area's lakes or work out at local fitness centers.

We contend that the institutional church of the twenty-first century cannot compete with these and other rivals for the hearts and minds of younger, secular Americans. It will lose every time. For example, would a typical young person rather go to a struggling, dwindling church on Sunday or stay at home and watch the Cowboys? Many of them opt for football or a trip to the shopping mall every time. Others see Sundays as a chance for a little time with the family at the beach, an opportunity to put in a little overtime at the office, or a chance to clean up the yard or catch up on housekeeping.

Where Churches Are at Fault

Donald Messer tells of a cartoon that portrays two young men sitting in the sun, wearing their baseball caps backward, as is the custom with many American youths. One kid looks at the other and remarks, "Somebody ought to invent a cap that would give a guy some shade!"[8] This image captures the essence of why so many churches aren't reaching people effectively. Like the teenagers with their backward baseball caps, these churches seem to have forgotten their original purpose—their mission to "make disciples" (Matt. 28:19–20). The following sections will examine three ways in which the church "has its hat on backward."

Churches Refuse to Change Their Methods

A visit to some churches is like a step back in time. If a young person in the early twenty-first century wants to know what life was like in America back in the early to mid-twentieth century, all he or she has to do is visit a church in the community. Although few other institutions or organizations reflect those times, you can count on the church to be there.

Some people compare attending a typical church service with experiencing a time warp similar to that found in Michael Crichton's book *Jurassic Park* and Stephen Spielberg's movie of the same title. "Eutychus" of *Christianity Today* describes such a visit:

> Welcome to Jurassic Park Denomination. You are now entering the lost world of the prehistoric past. Our tour begins in the board library. Here we notice two rare species. First the board member always pushing for more exegetical sermons from the Old Testament, the **bron-Torah-saurus.** Next to him you can see this creature's rival, the board member who likes lighter sermons, the **triceratopical.** On the right you can see the board member who loves to study the end times, **velocirapture.** Next, we proceed to the church kitchen. Here we find a board member who loves grazing at potlucks, socials, and outdoor picnics, the **barbequesaurus.**[9]

His approach, of course, is satirical, but real problems exist in the church's methodology or how it "does church." So many people in our churches are convinced that we must conduct church the way we've always done it. As one old-timer (the traditionasaurus) put it, "If the organ and the great hymns of the faith were good enough for Jesus and Paul, they must be good enough for us!" Bill Easum writes,

> Like the dinosaur, they have a voracious appetite. Much of their time, energy, and money is spent foraging for food, so that little time is left to feed the unchurched. . . . Food is everywhere. But many refuse to change their methods and structures to minister to people where they are in ways they can understand. Like the dinosaur, their necks are too stiff or their eyes too nearsighted.[10]

Easum concludes, "Congregations must deal with their stiff necks or their nearsightedness, or go the way of the dinosaur."[11] Some congregations will wake up in time to deal with their situations. Their necks will soften and their eyesight will be corrected. We call this process refocusing or revitalizing the church. Others will wake up, but it will be too late. However, too many will never wake up and will simply pass from the scene, much like the dinosaur.

We understand how difficult it is to change. For many people, the church is the one place they can go and count on it being the same week after week, in contrast to the world of work, which changes every other day. However, our church leaders must think about others as well as themselves. A case in point is ministry to our youth—the future of the church. If we don't adapt our methods to meet the needs of emerging generations, in time we'll have no younger generation in the church. No youth means no future. George Barna issues this warning:

> Faith is just one component in people's lives that helps them to interpret and cope with reality—and it certainly is not the central shaping influence for most people. The data regarding young adults also pose the possibility that churches are losing ground in terms of influence and may need to consider new approaches to making ancient truths more vivid and comprehensible in a technology-drenched, relativistic global community.[12]

The question that every church faces is this: What can or must change, and what must never change? The answer is found in one's theology of change. This is the crux of the problem for all churches generally and the American church particularly. We'll discuss this topic in more detail in chapter 4, but for now suffice it to say that the church can flex in its forms but not in its functions. Scripture dictates what the church must do (functions) but not how it does it (forms). This is not to suggest that the church must change its message if that message is based on the Bible. But the church must rethink how it communicates the biblical message. Our view is that most churches and their leadership, including the clergy, haven't thought through this issue. In a time when change is the only constant, it's imperative for the church to develop and follow a biblical theology of change.

Churches Have Failed to Take Advantage of Their Opportunities

Churches that have their hats on backward neither see nor take advantage of God-given opportunities. Scripture teaches that God is sovereign over the universe (Acts 4:24–29) and that He uses all events, good or bad, for the good of those who love Him and have been called according to His purpose (Rom. 8:28). This means that the various events in people's lives aren't happenstance. When these events occur, churches must ask, "How can we use these events to glorify God and reach out to those who are affected by them?"

A case in point is the terrorist attacks of September 11, 2001. This tragic event that has changed America in so many ways raises two strategic questions that the church must consider. First, how did the people that the churches are trying to reach respond to this event? Second, how did the church respond to them?

The answer to the first question is that a number of people who had never attended a church, or who had stopped attending, went to church the Sunday following the attacks. A Gallup poll reported that 47 percent of the adults surveyed on September 21–22, 2001, said that they had attended church or synagogue the previous week. This number was the highest since the 1950s.[13] The Barna Research Group reported that 48 percent of adults surveyed in late October and early November of 2001 said that they had attended a church service during the previous week, in contrast to 42 percent of adults polled between late July and early to mid-August. Barna also noted an increase in their concern about the future. In November 2001, 82 percent of adults in the Barna survey said that they were concerned about the future, compared to 73 percent in August.[14] Barna added that the population segment that expressed the most concern was adults age thirty-five and younger, among whom nearly nine out of ten expressed concern.[15]

Social scientists and analysts have discovered that most people turn to religion in times of national crisis and instability. Few evangelical Christians doubt that God used the attacks on September 11 to wake up Americans in general and the churches in particular to people's need for God and the church's role in helping them connect with Him. People responded to the crisis as we might have expected; the issue is whether the church used this opportunity to connect people with the Savior.

Unfortunately, the evidence regarding the church's response isn't encouraging. A Gallup poll conducted from November 8 to 11 revealed that church attendance had dropped to 42 percent (which is about where it was before the attacks), down from 47 percent in late September.[16] Apparently, these people didn't "stick."

Regarding his post-September 11 survey, Barna believes that the results indicate that churches failed to help post-attack newcomers connect with or deepen their faith:

> After the attack, millions of nominally churched or generally irreligious Americans were desperately seeking something that would restore stability and a sense of meaning to life. Fortunately, many of them turned to the church. Unfortunately, few of them experienced anything that was sufficiently life-changing to capture their attention and their allegiance. They tended to appreciate the moments of comfort they received, but were unaware of anything sufficiently unique or beneficial as to redesign their lifestyle to integrate a deeper level of spiritual involvement. Our assessment is that churches succeeded at putting on a friendly face but failed at motivating the vast majority of spiritual explorers to connect with Christ in a more intimate or intense manner.[17]

What we discovered is that the church wasn't ready for this tragic event. Like so many other institutions, it was caught by surprise. However, unlike many others, such as firemen, policemen, the Red Cross, and many average citizens, the church failed to react well. It didn't use the tragedy strategically for spiritual advantage. In our increasingly dangerous and uncertain times, the church must learn to respond quickly and make a difference. We might argue that emergency-oriented organizations such as the New York Fire

Department, the New York Police Department, and the Red Cross are prepared for such disasters. The church must become an emergency-oriented organization, as well. In light of two recent opportunities (President Bush's faith-based initiatives and the terrorist attacks), Barna challenges the church with the following statement:

> These two events are a wake up call to church leaders, empha-sizing the particular need to enhance their efforts in the areas of outreach and discipleship. We may never again have such grand opportunities to reach the nation for Christ—but then, we may have an even greater opportunity tomorrow. How many churches have leaders and believers who are poised to take advantage of such a pending opportunity?[18]

Churches Don't Value Evangelism

In the conclusion to chapter 1, we quoted Thom Rainer to the ef-fect that "America is clearly becoming less Christian, less evangelized, and less churched. Yet too many of those in our churches seem oblivi-ous to this reality."[19] The problem is that the overwhelming majority of American churches aren't committed to evangelism.

In the spring of 2001, Rainer put together a team from the Billy Graham School of Missions, Evangelism, and Church Growth at the Southern Baptist Theological Seminary located in Louisville, Kentucky. The goal was to conduct research on the unchurched in America. The team came to a startling conclusion about the church's role in evan-gelism. Rainer writes, "Less than four percent of churches in America meet our criteria to be an effective evangelistic church. Only one per-son is reached for Christ each year for every eighty-five church mem-bers in America."[20]

Perhaps an analogy would help. Assume for a moment that we own an insurance company with eighty-five salespeople. How long would we be in business if as a group they sold only one policy per year? Maybe this analogy will give us a better idea of why so many churches are "going out of business."

For a long time, Baptists have been known for their evangelism. Traditionally, they've had a strong passion to reach our lost and dying world. How are they doing at the beginning of the new century? Barna reports that at the end of 2001 "just four out of ten adults attending a Baptist church shared their faith in Christ with a nonbeliever in the past year—less than the proportion of adherents of many other denominations."[21] This finding is most troubling to me because I (Aubrey) am currently a member of and an elder in a Baptist church outside Dallas.

For much of my life as a Christian, I've attended and at times pastored Bible churches. A significant number of students who attend schools such as Moody Bible Institute, Multnomah School of the Bible, and Dallas Theological Seminary graduate and minister in churches that over the years have become part of the Bible church movement. The churches that make up this movement are popularly known primarily for their sound exposition of the Bible. Word has it that if you want to learn the Bible, go to a Bible church.

But how are the Bible churches doing in evangelism? My experience is that they're not doing well. I know of some that have gone for years with no conversions. This fact is surprising because one would think that a movement that values teaching and studying the Bible would be strong in obeying the Bible, but such doesn't seem to be the case. One friend who was a pastor of a Bible church in Dallas attempted to introduce change that included targeting and evangelizing lost people. The former pastors of this church had been teaching the Bible for more than half a century. My friend showed me a letter from a complaining member who wrote that the most important thing is to teach the Bible! According to the very same Bible, that member was wrong. The mission of the church, according to Matthew 28:19–20, is to make disciples. That mission includes evangelism. However, I suspect that many churches hold views similar to that Bible church member.

One of the reasons why churches aren't doing evangelism is that their pastors don't value it—much less do it. Barna reports, "Just 12 percent of senior pastors say they have the spiritual gift of leadership, only 8 percent say they have the gift of evangelism; in contrast, two-thirds say they have the gift of teaching or preaching."[22] We don't have to have an evangelistic gift to share our faith. However, most often, those with the gift of evangelism value evangelism and are impassioned to share their faith.

We've looked at some churches that aren't sharing their faith and were unpleasantly surprised. When we look at those who *are* sharing their faith, we are pleasantly surprised. "After exploring the religious life of adults attending a variety of Protestant churches," reports the Barna Research Group, "only three types of churches—Pentecostal, Assemblies of God, and nondenominational churches—had a majority of adherents who had shared their faith in Christ with a non-Christian in the past year."[23] This finding is important because many of these believers are charismatic. Those who tend to pride themselves in not being charismatic tend to look down on charismatics for their so-called theological naïveté. However, there's a huge difference between being theologically naive and not obeying the clear teaching of Scripture.

It will be impossible for the church of Jesus Christ to revive itself and make a difference for the Savior in this world if the church doesn't obey the Great Commission and share its faith. It's imperative that churches face this issue and commit to their God-intended mission.

Questions for Reflection and Discussion

1. Where is your church in terms of change? Would a visit to your church be a Jurassic Park experience? What can you do about this? What *will* you do?
2. Does your church typically take advantage of its God-given opportunities to reach people? How did it respond to the September 11 terrorist attacks? Why?
3. Is your church committed to evangelism? On what basis do you make that assessment? Is it reaching lost people? If so, how many? If not, why not? What will you do about this?

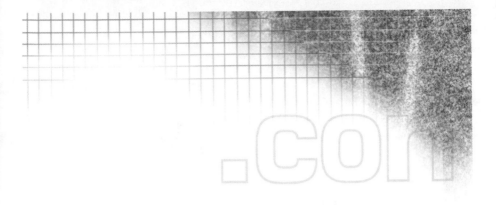

part two

The Solution: Reaching America's Generations

chapter three

Reaching New
Generations

Some older, traditional churches take pride in the fact that they're financially sound. Although they might be declining in size, they've been careful with their finances, and they have money in a savings account. If you were to ask someone on the board why they need a savings account, they would tell you that they're "saving up for a rainy day." It's likely that several old timers in the church and some who are on the board went through the Great Depression, when so many people struggled financially to survive. And they've learned their lesson well. Consequently, they've put aside funds in a savings account so that they don't get caught short if an emergency arises.

As a consultant and trainer, I (Aubrey) often work with declining churches that hope to breathe fresh life into their ministries. Sometimes they balk, however, at spending the funds necessary to accomplish spiritual revitalization. They have money in a savings account but not in the budget, because giving is down along with their attendance. If I ask why they can't use their savings, usually someone (such as the church treasurer) pipes up and says, "Because we're saving it for a rainy day." I like to follow up with the question, "Have you looked outside lately?"

The usual response is one of surprise followed by the question, "Why?"

My response is, "It's raining!"

As we've seen, the storm clouds of spiritual decline have been gathering for some time, and it's safe to say that rain is falling heavily on much of the American church. Far too many rain-soaked congregations are in serious decline and experiencing emergency conditions. Does this mean that the institutional church might go the way of the dinosaur and that Christianity could die along with it? The answer is unequivocally no. In Matthew 16:18, Jesus made a profound statement that breathes hope into all of us who embody His church: "I will build my church, and the gates of Hades will not overcome it." This doesn't mean that the typical "twentieth-century traditional" church as we've known it will survive. If a form or a certain way of "doing church" didn't survive in the first century, it won't survive in the twenty-first century either. It does mean, however, that Christ's church will survive.

The question then becomes, "What is the solution to the problems posed in part 1? How will the church survive? What must it do to bounce back and see sunny days ahead?" The rest of this book attempts to answer those questions. In this next section, we will propose a solution, and part 3 will address the methods that are vital to that solution.

To bounce back, the waterlogged American church must take three strategic steps. First, it must reach America's new, developing generations with the gospel. It seems the church is forever playing "catch up." About the time it begins to make some inroads into one generation, another generation comes along and catches it by surprise.

Second, to reach these new generations, the church must develop a theology of change—which is one of the larger struggles that the typical church faces. Most churches have become accustomed to doing church a certain way and are change-resistant. Many of them are afraid to implement change because they fear they might drift into heresy. Still others prefer the status quo. But every church needs a theology of change that will help them decide what can change and what must not.

Finally, the church must understand how the new generations think. Churches that find themselves behind the curve tend to be asking and answering the wrong questions. Theirs are the questions of a bygone era, not the spiritual questions that younger generations are asking. Adding to this problem, the nation seems to be shifting worldviews— from modernism to postmodernism. Younger generations think and act differently. Thus, the church should investigate postmodernism to understand its questions and to learn from those who are reaching the postmodern generation effectively.

Our purpose in this chapter is to address the church's pursuit of America's new generations. Ministry is all about people, and people tend to cluster in generations. William Strauss and Neil Howe explain that a generation is "the aggregate of all people born over roughly the span of a phase of life who share a common location in history and, hence, a common collective persona."[1] The span of a generation is roughly two decades, or twenty years, which means that three or four generations will be coexisting at any given time. We will view two new generations—the busters and the bridgers—in the context of two current, well-established generations—the builders and the boomers—because rather than being carbon copies of the preceding generations, as some forecasters assumed, each new generation has reacted to the preceding generations in new and different ways. Often, the emerging generations have sought to correct what they view as the faults of the current generations.

The Present: Reaching the Builder and the Baby Boom Generations

Christ's solution has always been and always will be the Great Commission, regardless of the generation. It's Christ's mission for His church and is found in several passages in the Scriptures. One is Mark 16:15: "He said to them, 'Go into all the world and preach the good news to all creation.'" The emphasis in this passage is evangelism in all of the world (in our terms, at home and abroad). Another such passage is Matthew 28:19–20: "Therefore go and make disciples of all nations, baptizing them in the name of the Father and of the Son and of the Holy Spirit, and teaching them to obey everything I have commanded you." This reference emphasizes evangelism *and* edification, in the form of teaching and obedience. This is our message for reaching every generation. However, we begin here with America's current generations—the builders and the boomers.

Reaching the Builder Generation

Demographics

The builder generation comprises those Americans born before 1943. It encompasses the G. I. generation (born 1901–1924) and the silent generation (born 1925–1942).[2] In 2003, builders range in age from sixty-one to one-hundred-two years old—approximately fifty million people who make up less than 18 percent of the population.[3] The majority of this generation is retired or close to retirement.

Core Values

Builders have always valued dedication and sacrifice, as displayed by their involvement in the two world wars. They've been willing to delay rewards, putting duty before pleasure. In their heyday, they were hard workers who believed in earning a living, and now they are enjoying the fruit of their labor while living in retirement. Also, they respect authority, which means that they're law-and-order people. Finally, builders place a high premium on logic and reason to the extent that builder men don't trust their emotions and are suspicious of anything emotional.

Characteristics

This generation fought three wars (World War I, World War II, and the Korean War). Initially, it experienced a financial boom followed by a stock market crash and the Great Depression. The latter event triggered the New Deal revolution that, in turn, led to a vast expansion of the federal government. Subsidized by the G. I. Bill, many of these people went to college, built the suburbs, invented miracle vaccines (such as the polio vaccine), and later launched rockets to the moon.

Builders like to think big. They envisioned one great society where people assumed that all would be well. Consequently, they built things big—big businesses, big governments, and big unions. Generally, many of them preferred to work faithfully for large corporations that offered generous retirement plans. Their goal was to work for the same business much of their life, then retire and enjoy their retirement. Many of them have accomplished their goals, making them the most affluent of all of the generations.

Personalities

Some well-known builders are presidents John Kennedy and Ronald Reagan, actors John Wayne and Jimmy Stewart, news anchorman Walter Cronkite, civil rights activist Martin Luther King Jr., military leader Colin Powell, sports figures Joe DiMaggio and Vince Lombardi, and singer Elvis Presley.

The Church

How did the builder-generation church minister for Christ? In addition to big businesses, government, and trade unions, builders built big denominations that built big churches. They directed the largest expansion of mainline and conservative denominational churches in the twentieth century. Many of the large downtown "first churches" are monuments to the builder generation.

The church's primary strategy is summarized by the words *three to thrive,* which refers to the thrice weekly meeting schedule of these congregations. This model still exists in some of the large, older churches, but it is more often seen in the smaller, evangelical, traditional churches that are the backbone of the American church. The typical white, nonliturgical church met twice on Sunday and once during the week. It met on Sunday morning, beginning with Sunday school and followed by a worship service. Sunday school served several purposes, depending on the denomination or organization. For some churches, it was a time to teach believers the truths of the Bible. For other churches, such as the Baptists, it was a time for evangelism. The worship event usually consisted of singing several great hymns of the faith followed by a prayer and a sermon that ranged from forty-five minutes to an hour in length. The sermon might vary from a gospel presentation to a Bible message that included a gospel presentation.

Members were encouraged to come back on Sunday evening for a second worship service that most often focused on a message from God's Word. It might include gospel singing. The church would meet again at midweek for prayer, and the midweek service might include a short devotional. Some churches scheduled special events for the kids on Sunday or Wednesday evenings.

Attendance was usually largest on Sunday morning, but trailed off on Sunday nights; only the "faithful" showed up for the Wednesday night prayer meeting. In an effort to get more people out to the services, well-intentioned individuals would exhort their people with the following: "You can tell how many people love the church by those who come on Sunday mornings, and you can tell how many love the pastor by those who come on Sunday evenings. But you can tell who loves the Lord by those who come to Wednesday night prayer meeting. See you Wednesday night."

African-American churches also flourished during this period. Typically, they met for a longer time, often starting at 11:00 A.M. and going well into the early afternoon. Many of them functioned not only to evangelize and preach the Bible but also to serve as centers for political life that encouraged the enfranchisement of the black community.

During this time, the Gallup organization began to track American church attendance. The first survey in 1939 found that the nation's average church attendance was a low 39 percent. However, from 1954 to 1962, the builder generation was responsible for the highest church attendance ever recorded, an average of 48 percent. Apparently, over time, the three-services approach resulted in some thriving churches, at least during the 1950s and 1960s.

Reaching the Baby-Boom Generation

Demographics

The baby-boom generation followed the builder generation. It consists of Americans born between 1943 and 1960. Currently, they range in age from forty-three to sixty and make up approximately 24 percent of the population, numbering around sixty-six million people. The boomers represent the "boom" of births that followed the return of U.S. servicemen at the conclusion of World War II.

Core Values

The core values of this generation are optimism and idealism; consequently, they were convinced they could make this country a better place in which to live. They believe in teamwork and prefer to work together. They are also committed to change what they believe to be unjust, often bureaucratic rules and laws. They value experimentation and are open to taking risks and trying new things. They pursue health and wellness and, unlike the builders, put pleasure before duty.

Characteristics

The baby-boom generation witnessed America's ascendance as a global superpower. They experienced the financial prosperity of the builders, but objected to a huge peacetime defense budget that funded a cold war economy. Many of them grew up nurtured by Dr. Spock in Beaver Cleaver families where father knows best. They came of age in the 1960s, rebelling against their parents and a government that fought what the boomers believed was an unjust war in Vietnam. They also accused the government of nurturing a racist, politically corrupt society at home. During the 1960s, civil rights became a prominent issue with numerous demonstrations taking place in many parts of America. Boomers also birthed the sexual revolution, viewing themselves as arbiters of public morality who preferred to make love instead of war.

In recent years, however, this generation has mellowed considerably. For example, some of the radicals who were so against "the system" in the 1960s have become "respectable" citizens and business people who now embrace and make up the system.

Personalities

Some popular boomers are former president Bill Clinton, sports figures Joe Namath and John McEnroe, comedian Spike Lee, singer Janis Joplin, comedian David Letterman, and entrepreneurs Steve Jobs and Bill Gates.

The Church

Although we have painted a bleak picture of a traditional church that has been staggering over the past twenty to thirty years, the boomer generation has developed some notable and delightful exceptions. Perhaps the most influential church of the last two decades is Willow Creek Community Church in Barrington, Illinois (a suburb of Chicago). Bill Hybels and a team of young people launched this cutting-edge church in 1975 with a vision of reaching unchurched seekers, whom they affectionately labeled "unchurched Harry and Mary." Over the past twenty-eight years, many thousands of churches nationwide and some overseas have studied the Willow Creek model and sought to adapt the seeker concept to their ministries. What has made this way of doing church so refreshing is that it seeks to create a Great Commission church that reaches out to unchurched people rather than "holing up" within the four walls of the church with "our kind of people."

In an attempt to partner with their congregation in reaching the lost, Willow Creek has developed a seven-step strategy. One step that has received perhaps the most attention is their setting aside Sunday morning as a "seeker service" that presents basic Christianity in ways that make it clear and relevant to the lost. Willow Creek's staff and committed volunteers regularly encourage their people to invite and bring their unchurched friends to this service.

As happens to most new movements that God uses to breathe fresh life into the church, Willow Creek has its critics. For example, some pastors and seminary professors have criticized the Sunday morning "seeker service," claiming that Scripture teaches that Sunday morning is a worship time for believers. The problem with that view is three-fold. First, the passages they use (such as Acts 20:7; 1 Cor. 16:2; Rev. 1:10) are descriptive, not prescriptive. Second, nowhere does the Bible teach that the church must meet for worship on Sunday or the first day of the week. In fact, Romans 14:5–11 gives the church liberty as to when it meets. Third, Willow Creek is practicing Philippians 2:4, where Paul exhorts, "Each of you should look not only to your own interests, but also to the interests of others." Then Paul proceeds to identify this attitude with that of the Savior.[4]

During the 1980s through 2000, a number of churches and denominations planted churches. Denominations, in particular, realized that if they didn't launch new churches, they would become extinct. Believing that it takes new kinds of churches to reach new kinds of people, boomer pastors also launched a number of new paradigm churches. These idealistic believers sought new forms of worship, jettisoning what was for them older, traditional forms that stifled believers and "turned off" unbelievers. These and other churches have taught us that it takes all kinds of churches to reach all kinds of people. They've also brought us hope for the future and taught us that the church can still be vital and relevant to one's generation.

The Future: Reaching the Buster and the Bridger Generations

I (Aubrey) have been training church planters at Dallas Seminary for the past twenty years, and I've also written a book on church planting that has been used widely across America and beyond. My current concern for church planting in the twenty-first century is that it's geared primarily to reach baby boomers. The baby-boom churches are making the same mistakes that their builder parents made. They're so focused on the present that they're missing the future. On the one hand, the church has made some inroads to reaching unchurched boomers; on the other hand, it's about to miss the opportunity to reach busters and bridgers.

Early in the summer of 2000, a significant demographic event took place without any fanfare. All of the news agencies missed it. According to the U.S. Census Bureau, the number of people who are thirty-five and under (142,174,980) exceeded the number of those who are over thirty-five (142,092,916).[5] In other words, the newer generations—the busters and the bridgers—now outnumber the established generations—the builders and the boomers.

What does this shift in population signal for the church? While it's imperative that the church continue to minister to and love its older people, the future of the church is its young people. Statistically, the probability of reaching someone for Christ diminishes after age nineteen. Barna reports that two-thirds of people under age thirty-five shun all organized religion.[6] If the church in America is to make a significant difference in the twenty-first century, it must begin to target and reach the future generations as well as the current generations.

Reaching the Buster Generation

Demographics

The busters followed the boomers on America's generational scene. Also known as Gen Xers and the Thirteenth Generation, the busters are those people born between 1961 and 1981. Ranging in age from twenty-two to forty-forty, they make up slightly less than 30 percent of the population, approximately eighty-three million people. Consequently, they outnumber the boomer generation.

Where did they get the name *busters?* Everyone has struggled to come up with a name for this generation. One thought is that the idealistic boomers labeled this next generation "busters" because, in their opinion, they've proven to be a bust in contrast to all the boomer accomplishments. More likely, however, is the simple explanation that in 1965 the birthrate dropped below 3.8 million per year, a trend that continued through 1976.

Core Values

Busters comprise a techno-literate generation that is very much into computers. They value diversity at home while thinking globally. They are somewhat informal, as reflected by their piercings, tattoos, unkempt hair, and excessively baggy pants. Busters very much value life; they work to live, not live to work.

Characteristics

Busters have the reputation of being a negative, somewhat cynical generation. This characteristic might be reflected in their music, which ranges from grunge to hip-hop. If this is true, it's because so many of them grew up quickly as latchkey kids with divorced parents. As young adults, they've faced a society that promotes sexual promiscuity that has been tempered somewhat by an AIDS epidemic. At work, they are free-agent risk takers who prefer to work independently rather than to be loyal to a single corporation. Having embraced computers in high school and college, most of them are proficient with them, using them at home and in their employment. Contrary to the builders, who might have worked for the same company for life, busters are more likely to work for one company for three to five years and then move on to another company. The busters have proved to be cynics in their encounters with leaders; they don't trust them. They are suspicious of anyone, whether in politics or religion, who claims to be a leader. They are politically and religiously pragmatic; for busters, *doing* is more important than *believing*.

Personalities

Well-known busters include actors Tom Cruise, Brooke Shields, and Jodie Foster; comedian Eddie Murphy; entrepreneur Michael Dell; singer Jon Bon Jovi; sports figures Deion Sanders and Mike Tyson; and film maker Quentin Tarantino.

The Church

Church attendance is a low priority for busters. Barna estimates that only 34 percent of busters attend church in a typical week, and that figure might be generous.[7] This is 7 percent lower than the boomers (41 percent) and 17 percent lower than the builders (51 percent).[8]

The busters have taken a decided departure from their boomer predecessors. Churches that reach busters differ from the Willow Creek model and other contemporary faith communities in several ways. Although some busters participate in megachurches, most seem to prefer smaller churches, which some people call the microchurch. According to a comprehensive survey by the Hartford Institute for Religious Research, approximately 50 percent of America's churches have fewer than one hundred adults in attendance, and another full quarter of them have fewer than fifty adults. Some of those churches were once larger but have dwindled to their current size.

Second, the hallmark of faith for this generation is authenticity experienced in the context of community. Authenticity is being the same from core to crust. It concerns living out what is on the inside. Community is the context in which busters experience authenticity. Whereas boomers are apt to slip into and out of services undetected, busters prefer to hang out and spend time together. Two hours after a service, you might find them still hanging around, talking.

Third, busters worship differently than boomers. Rather than creating new-paradigm, contemporary churches, they have taken a more traditional approach. Some traditionalists believe that busters have embraced the builder's traditional church model, made in the image of the Reformation. Actually, they've skipped over the Reformation, moving back to a style of worship more like that of the first few centuries. Their service often meets in the evening. Their worship consists of a message from the Bible and the liturgy, often set in the context of votive candles. They might pray the Lord's Prayer and recite a creed. Some of them have also embraced the weekly serving of the Lord's Supper. Also, a number of buster churches are adding new forms of artistic expression along with corporate readings.

What's going on here? Why the drastic contrast with the boomer's approach to church? One explanation is that it's a "God thing." This is how God happens to be working with and through the buster generation. It's a mystery, so don't even attempt to explain it. Another explanation is that the busters lack a sense of family and connectedness. Far too many of them have grown up in single-parent homes without any sense of family or extended relationships. And what's happening is that in their own way, they're "putting down roots" as they build their own traditions.

Reaching the Bridger Generation

Demographics

The bridgers are the generation that follows the busters. Popularly known as millennials and Generation Y, the bridgers were born between 1982 and the present.[9] Ranging in age up to twenty-one years old, they number around eighty-three million people and, like the busters, make up approximately 30 percent of the population. Combined with the buster population, they outnumber the builder and boomer generations. Thom Rainer coined the term *bridger* because this generation is the bridge to the twenty-first century and the new millennium.[10]

Core Values

Bridgers hold such values as optimism, confidence, diversity, making money, personal achievement, good manners, civic involvement, and a strong moral code.

Characteristics

Contrary to the more cynical busters, the bridgers are more optimistic with hope for the future. They're also more group driven, wanting to work together and help one another. They're civic-minded doers; they want to do their part to contribute to society. Some of the issues they face are not new: leadership, guns and crime, environmental issues, racism, and problems in education.

They've grown up in a multiracial, multicultural world. A number of them have parents of different races, and a majority of them from ages twelve to seventeen respect members of minority racial and ethnic groups.[11] However, the nation's neighborhoods and schools continue to be segregated, and that is a cause of concern for many bridgers.

Unlike the busters, they respect authority and turn to a parent or parents for general guidance and answers to their questions. They've not experienced the kind of generation gap that has characterized the boomers and the busters. We say "a parent or parents" because only about half of the bridgers have grown up or will grow up with both biological parents present in the home.

They aren't as artistic as the busters, nor are they the lonely, creative types—poets and painters. They've also left behind the piercings and tattoos of their predecessors. However, they're as technologically savvy as the busters and either were computer literate by the time they began school or were introduced to computers in primary or secondary schools. Another name for bridgers is the Internet generation, because they spend much of their time online. Some of them, including my granddaughter, have their own Web sites. A recent study of twelve- to seventeen-year-olds states that about 73 percent of U.S. teenagers use the Internet and say that it plays a significant role in their relationships with their family and friends.[12]

Personalities

Well-known bridgers include Jessica McClure, Mary Kate and Ashley Olsen, Elisa Lopez, Baby "M," Dooney Waters, and Tabatha Foster.

The Church

The bridger generation is the most unchurched generation of the past one hundred years. Barna reports that approximately 29 percent attend a church, and that figure might be high.[13] Barna Research adds that "these young people have the lowest likelihood of being involved in church life when they are older and living independently of any 'class' of teenagers surveyed . . . since 1981."[14] Rainer states that his recent research on teenage bridgers indicates that only 4 percent understand the gospel and have accepted Christ, even if they attend church.[15]

In light of the preceding statistics, it's surprising that, in *The Bridger Generation*, Rainer points out that the bridgers are perhaps more religious than any other generation in the twentieth century. However, he explains, by "religious" he means that they believe in almost any expression of a higher power. For bridgers, *what* you believe isn't as important as believing *something*. They're a generation that has been schooled not to believe in absolutes; thus, they resist any claim that one faith is true in contrast to another.[16]

Rainer wisely expresses his concern that Islam is the church's primary competition for the hearts and souls of this generation.[17] And after the September 11 terrorist attacks, America's interest in Islam has skyrocketed.

As the church seeks to reach both the bridgers and the busters in the twenty-first century, it must think and act strategically. Regardless of the generation or its culture, certain concepts make up the DNA of any church and help it to minister strategically. They are its core values, mission, vision, and strategy for ministry. Core values, mission, and vision won't change much. However, strategies must change to take into consideration matters of generational culture. Today's church must examine both the bridger and the buster cultures and ask, "What are some ways that God can use His church to make inroads into these generations with Christ's gospel?" In light of the bridgers' voracious interest in and use of the Internet, we believe that the church must use this technology as a primary means for reaching the generation. This will be the subject of chapters 6 through 8.

Questions for Reflection and Discussion

1. Approximately what percentage of your church is made up of builders, boomers, busters, and bridgers?
2. If your church consists primarily of builders, how will this affect its future? If it consists primarily of builders and boomers, what might this say about its future?
3. The combined size of the buster and bridger generations is now larger than the builder and boomer generations combined. How will this new reality affect the future of the church in general and the future of American Christianity in particular?
4. Does your church have many busters and bridgers? If so, why? If not, why not?
5. How serious is your church about reaching busters and bridgers? To what extent will you go to reach out to them and minister to their needs? Is your church willing to change its current ministry to reach these generations? Would you be willing to create an alternative service exclusively for them (a church within a church)? Would you be willing to plant a church that targets busters and bridgers specifically?

chapter four

Developing a
Theology of Change

Perhaps you've heard the story of the college freshman who stopped a young lady who was hurrying to class. He asked, "What's the rush?"

She responded, "I want to get to class before my new textbook goes out of date!"

Few people would disagree that change is now taking place at a faster rate than anytime in the past. Michael Gerber writes, "Today's world is a difficult place. Mankind has experienced more change in the past twenty years than in the two thousand that preceded them."[1] George Barna indicates that "our culture completely reinvents itself every three to five years."[2] Another authority has calculated that the field of knowledge doubles every eighteen months.[3] There is little question that change has become an enduring constant, both locally and globally. And with the current explosion of information technology, all indications are that "we ain't seen nothin' yet."

Although we know that the world is changing, we also know the church isn't coping well with that change. But even those churches that balk at change can't avoid it. The problem for many of our faith communities is that they don't seem to understand that change can be either bad or good. They assume that all change is bad and therefore tend to resist it. Consequently, change when it does occur affects them adversely. The questions we ought to be asking ourselves are these: How can the church handle change more effectively? How can it handle change so that it glorifies God and accomplishes Christ's Great

Commission? This chapter will attempt to answer these questions by first exploring the problem of change and then suggesting a solution.

The Problem: Understanding That It's Okay to Change

As we look at the church's general resistance to change, we want to focus attention on two specific questions: Do churches need to change? and How do churches view change?

Do Churches Need to Change?

Churches require at least two things to survive—people and money. A church isn't a facility with grounds—it's people. Without people, all you have is an empty building, not a church. However, those people have to support the church with their finances. Nobody likes to admit it, but the church has a corporate side. It's a corporate community with a cause. And it's the corporate side that must contend with such mundane matters as finances. Most churches have a mortgage, a payroll, monthly bills for the utilities, and other financial obligations.

If church attendance is erratic at best—or, worse, declining, it's no surprise that church finances would be erratic or declining, as well. Although most people still say that religion is very important in their lives, if they "vote with their feet" instead of with their pocketbooks, the institutional church cannot sustain itself. Some churches have already closed their doors, and I predict that more will follow. When I work with declining churches, I ask them to conduct a ministry analysis that will show how their church is doing and why. Two things I evaluate are the percentage of decline in attendance and the percentage of decline in giving. I can usually get their attention when I combine these two factors and predict within months when the church will have to close its doors.

As these churches dwindle, it doesn't take a Nobel laureate economist to predict that their finances will dwindle with them. As the builder generation—the most affluent generation of the twentieth century—continues to age and die over the next decade, we will see an accelerating shift of financial assets to their children. These suc-ceeding generations are largely unchurched, and they're not interested in the church. Thus, much of the funding that builders have gener-ously contributed to the church will likely be diverted elsewhere. Con-sequently, churches and denominations that have depended on support from the builders will have to rethink how they're going to finance their ministries.

An even bigger issue is the immediacy of the problem. Churches not only need to change, they need to change *now*. "At the risk of sounding like an alarmist," says George Barna, "I believe the Church in America has no more than five years—perhaps even less—to turn itself around and begin to affect the culture, rather than be affected by it. Because our culture completely reinvents itself every three to five years, . . . we have no more than a half-decade to turn things around."[4]

We don't have much time to think about solutions. We can't put this off until another day. We must think and act now.

How Do Churches View Change?

The second problem is the church's view of change. Although a growing number of congregations are beginning to discover and ac-knowledge the need for change, they aren't sure that it's okay to change. Is changing "the way we do things around here" biblical? That is the central issue. If we begin to implement changes in the church, will we diminish the gospel? Are we subtly slipping into heresy?

Of all of the reasons for a church to be cautious about change, the risk of heresy is the most compelling. Church decline, the increase in the number of unchurched, and the growth of cults and nonreligious groups doesn't mean that the church should change if that would mean abandoning the faith. Some people argue that it will lead to that re-sult, pointing to what has happened to the faith of the mainline churches. If this is the case, as some people fear, then change is out of the question. Consequently, in the rest of this chapter, we'll deal with the theological issue of change.

The Solution: Helping Churches
Develop a Theology of Change

Even the most diehard opponents of change agree that the church must change in some ways. Biblically, the heart of the issue is legitimate change; what can change and what can't? To answer this question, it's imperative for the church to develop and follow a theology of change, which includes three concepts: function, form, and freedom.

The Church's Functions

We can best understand the church's function if we define our terms and provide some biblical examples.

A THEOLOGY OF CHANGE

Categories	Functions	Forms
Characteristics	Timeless, unchanging, nonnegotiable precepts	Timely, changing, negotiable practices
Basis	Scripture	Culture
Usage	Mandates	Methods
Implication	All churches must pursue	All churches are free to choose
Purpose	Accomplishes the church's purpose	Accomplishes the church's functions

Table 1

The *functions* of the church are timeless, unchanging, nonnegotiable precepts based on Scripture. They are the biblical mandates that determine what every church must pursue in order to accomplish its purpose.

The first important element of the church's functions is *timelessness.* The same specific functions that characterized the church in the first century must also characterize the church in the twenty-first century. And should Christ not return in the twenty-first century, the church's functions will lead it into the twenty-second century. One example of a timeless function is evangelism. Faith communities have practiced evangelism since the first century, and the Savior expects us to perform the same function of evangelism in the twenty-first century (Matt. 28:19–20; Mark 16:15). As long as there is a church, it will have functions.

Another characteristic of functions is that they *don't change.* Developing a theology of change will force us to differentiate between those things that must change, and those that must never change. One thing that must never change is the church's functions. The Holy Spirit inspired the writing of the New Testament, which prescribes certain functions for the church. It doesn't matter how many other changes come our way, the church must not abandon its functions. The mistake that the mainline churches made was in changing their functions. When cultural changes swept over them, they decided to abandon Christ's functions and implemented their own ideas, such as the denial of the inspiration and authority of Scripture, the legitimization of the homosexual lifestyle, the ordination of homosexuals, and the acceptance of all faiths—Christian or non-Christian—as legitimate under God.

A third characteristic of functions is that they are *nonnegotiable.* The churches of the first century couldn't pick and choose what they wanted to believe, and neither can churches in the twenty-first century. To function biblically, the church should pursue *all* of its functions. The niche church phenomenon, wherein churches specialize in particular functions, flies in the face of the church's mandated functions. Christ didn't commission some churches to be family churches, others to be counseling centers, and still others to be strong in fellowship or worship or teaching. Christ commands His church to make disciples, not niches.

Scripture is the basis or foundation for all of the church's functions. In 2 Timothy 3:16–17, Paul writes, "All Scripture is God-breathed and is useful for teaching, rebuking, correcting and training in righteousness, so that the man of God may be thoroughly equipped for every good work." Consequently, the Bible must support the church's functions. For example, we find several of the church's functions in Acts 2:42–47. Although this passage is descriptive of the ministry of the Jerusalem church, other passages prescribe each function for the church.

A third element is how functions are used. Timeless, unchanging functions are the church's mandate. They aren't options; they detail for us our ministry precepts. For example, early in the twenty-first century, an old, tired, rain-soaked church isn't doing much evangelism. The problem is that evangelism is not an option. Thus, every church would be wise to note the biblical functions and use them to evaluate how they're doing. They are the keys to church health.

Some people may contend that this is legalism. But it's not legalism to obey the church's mandates; it's legalism when a church mandates what isn't a biblical precept. I'll say more about this in the section on freedom.

We must also consider the implications of the church's functions. As long as the church continues to ignore functions such as evangelism, it will not serve Christ's mission. In short, it will be a disobedient church. One group responded to these strong words by saying, "But we teach the Bible; the most important thing is the Bible!"

In one sense, the most important thing *is* the Bible, because not only is it the foundation for what we believe but it also identifies the functions we're to follow. But what the protesting church missed is that God expects us to *obey* the Bible. The implication is that we're not only to be hearers of the Word but also doers of the Word (James 1:22–25). The church's "marching orders" state that the church is to teach its people to obey everything that Christ commanded (Matt. 28:20). It's wonderful that these Christians love the teaching of the Scriptures; no one should fault them for that. However, it is equally important that they obey the Scriptures.

All of the functions serve a common purpose. Functions such as fellowship, evangelism, worship, and the rest work together to accomplish God's purpose for His church—His glorification (1 Cor. 10:31).

What Are Some Examples of Functions?

Like so many other things in the Scriptures, defining the church's biblical functions is open to interpretation. In Acts 2:42–47, Luke describes, though not exhaustively, some of the functions that characterized the young, biblically functioning, spiritually healthy Jerusalem church:

> They devoted themselves to the apostles' teaching and to the fellowship, to the breaking of bread and to prayer. Everyone was filled with awe, and many wonders and miraculous signs were done by the apostles. All the believers were together and had everything in common. Selling their possessions and goods, they gave to anyone as he had need. Every day they continued to meet together in the temple courts. They broke bread in their homes and ate together with glad and sincere hearts, praising God and enjoying the favor of all the people. And the Lord added to their number daily those who were being saved.

In verse 42, Luke mentions four functions of the church. The first function is the apostle's teaching—what some people refer to as doctrine, or the teachings of the Bible. The second function is fellowship, which emphasizes the importance of Christians spending time with other Christians. Although we should spend time with unbelievers, we must also spend time with other believers, or we'll begin to drift away from the faith. The third function is the breaking of bread, which could refer to eating together but is probably a technical term for the Lord's Supper, or Communion. And the fourth function is prayer, which is vital to the church's spiritual life.

Several other functions are sprinkled throughout the rest of the passage, one of which is community, which refers to such matters as sharing possessions and finances to meet both the material and the spiritual needs of others (vv. 44–45). Another function is worship, which, in this context, involves praising God (v. 47). Yet another function is evangelism (v. 47). Actually, one could argue that the functions begin in verse 41 with evangelism and end in verse 47 with evangelism. Evangelism serves as "functional bookends" for this section.

Acts 2:42–47 describes what the Jerusalem church practiced, but practice isn't the same as precept. However, each function mentioned in Acts 2 is found as a precept elsewhere in Scripture. For example, in Colossians 4:2, Paul directs the church to pray. In 2 Timothy 4:2, he commands Timothy to "preach the Word," which could refer to either teaching the apostle's doctrine or evangelism (Acts 8:4–5). And community is the precept behind the numerous "one another" passages that are sprinkled throughout the New Testament.

How Do We Discover the Functions?

One way to discover the functions, as we've already noted, is to look for biblical mandates or precepts. If Paul instructs the church to pray, as he does in Colossians 4:2 and 1 Thessalonians 5:17, then it's a function. Therefore, numerous functions—some more important than others—are prescribed for the church in Scripture.

A second way to discover the functions is to understand that functions are ends rather than means to an end. Let's return to evangelism as an example. Evangelism can be done in numerous ways. Those are evangelistic means. However, the end for all of these means is the evangelism or conversion of souls to Christ.

Another way to articulate this point is to say that the functions explain why the church does what it does. As we'll see shortly, what the church *does* is its forms. Behind the forms, however, are its functions. The church might have a very active small-groups ministry. Small groups are what the church does, a ministry form or method. But why does the church have such a program? In this case, it's to promote biblical community, which is an important church function.

The Church's Forms

A second concept that is critical to developing and implementing a theology of change is a ministry's *forms*. We can best understand the concept of forms if we define it, provide some examples, and then discuss how to discover or identify some church forms.

Forms are the temporal, changing, negotiable practices, based on the church's culture and methods, that all churches are free to choose in order to accomplish their functions. Several elements make up this definition.

Unlike functions, forms are not timeless; they're timely or temporal. Whereas functions are the same today as they were in the first century, the forms they take will be context sensitive. First-century forms aren't necessarily twenty-first century forms. The first-century church met in homes or house churches (Acts 2:46; 8:3; 12:12). They also met in the temple (Acts 2:46) or Solomon's Colonnade (Acts 3:11; 5:12). The twenty-first century church might meet in homes, but more often meets in a building that we call "the church." It would be most difficult to meet today in the temple or Solomon's Colonnade.

To be effective, forms must be *changeable*. That's part of being context sensitive. Today's church leaders would be wise to observe and learn from the men of Issachar, "who understood the times and knew what Israel should do" (1 Chron. 12:32). Observing and understanding the times and then making decisions about what the church will do is being context-sensitive and culturally current. If the people whom we're trying to reach for Christ are reluctant to meet in small groups in homes, for example, then we would be wise to select another site, possibly a building.

This is where the mainline churches went wrong. They changed the biblical functions, denying the very basis of the Christian faith, but failed to change many of the forms. For example, their young people weren't turned off to Christ or the Scriptures, they were unhappy with such things as long, tedious sermons and traditional styles of worship. One common complaint was that they didn't understand the words to the hymns. Because these issues are matters of form, the church can and should do something if it is to reach and retain the younger generations.

Third, forms are also negotiable. We may discuss several options before we choose the forms that we believe will best serve our biblical functions as a church. We don't have to meet in homes or in a building, for example. We could meet outdoors. A better but more controversial example pertains to styles of worship. Contrary to what many people believe and teach, a church's choice of worship style—contemporary or traditional—is one of preference based on "understanding the times." Scripture doesn't mandate singing the great hymns of the faith accompanied by an organ or any other instrument. Nor does it mandate contemporary worship. A church that prefers a more traditional style of worship might minister more effectively to its young people by adding a contemporary service.

As we've seen, Scriptural mandates are the basis for the church's functions. By contrast, cultural context is the basis for its forms. The temptation for every church is that, over time, it may begin to equate its culturally relative forms and traditions with its functions. This isn't necessarily intentional. Once a form has been established over a long period, it's easy to think there's only one best way to practice a particular function. "The way we do things around here" begins to take on an almost biblical authority.

Some object strenuously to the concept of cultural relevance. They believe that we should bend the culture to conform to the church, rather than the other way around. But culture isn't bad. In a sense, it's neutral, a vehicle that can be used for either good or bad. For example, language is a key component of culture. Language can be used to praise God or curse Him (James 3:9). Jesus was relevant to his culture. He chose to dress like the people around Him, and He spoke their language. Otherwise, his clothing would have unnecessarily distracted from His message, and people wouldn't have understood His language.

Another way to understand forms is that they are the church's *methods* for ministry. A problem occurs when the church treats its forms as if they were mandates rather than means. Some people seem to assume, in defending their traditions, that whoever adopted the form to begin with must have based it on Scripture. The obvious solution is to look to the Scriptures. If we can't prove our position from the Scriptures (apart from proof-texting), then we must not insist on our preferences—or we should at least be open to new ideas. One reason so many young people are dropping out of church is because the older generations have unwisely insisted that the church do things the way they've always been done (according to the preferences of the leaders and the old guard) or they'll take their financial support somewhere else (which amounts to ecclesiastical blackmail). This attitude is unbiblical and un-Christian.

If the church's functions are biblical mandates to be followed by Christ's churches, and its forms are not biblical mandates but are based on culture, what are the implications of the forms we choose? In a nutshell, the church is free to choose the cultural forms that best communicate biblical truth to those who live in that culture. I will say more about this when we get to the concept of freedom. However, the church must exercise its freedom under the guidelines of godly wisdom. I question the wisdom of a pastor who would act in the first month of a new pastorate to eliminate a traditional worship style and replace it with a contemporary style (or vice versa), unless extenuating circumstances existed.

Finally, the church's functions aid it in accomplishing its purpose—to honor or glorify God. The purpose of the church's forms, however, is to aid it in accomplishing the church's functions. The architectural principle that form follows function is true for the church.

In 1 Corinthians 9:22, Paul writes, "To the weak I became weak, to win the weak. I have become all things to all men so that by all possible means I might save some." Paul's goal was to win people to Christ. However, he was willing to use whatever means would accomplish that goal. When the functions are in the driver's seat, where they should be, the church will first identify its functions and then ask what forms best accomplish those functions. We must remember that every form has a cultural "shelf life." They might powerfully and effectively accomplish the church's functions. However, when the culture changes, the church must be flexible enough to change with it.

How Do We Discover Some Examples of Forms?

It wouldn't be prudent in a work such as this to attempt to identify every form possible for all the biblical functions. Some forms haven't even been discovered yet. However, I believe that the church's leaders have the responsibility to be aware of not only the biblical functions but also the various forms that God is using to accomplish those functions.

One way to keep up with what God is doing is to scan the church environment to discover various ministry forms. To think and act strategically, churches must be cultural observers who survey the landscape in search of effective ways that God is using to work through churches in America and around the world to accomplish its biblically mandated functions. There are several ways to pursue this objective, one of which is to attend church conferences. Various churches in North America (such as Willow Creek; Saddleback Community Church in California; and Oak Cliff Bible Fellowship in Dallas, among others) sponsor church conferences at which they present, in effect, the forms they are using to accomplish biblical functions.

Another way to keep up with emerging forms is to monitor church Web sites. Leaders can learn much about other churches and their ministry practices by sifting through their Web sites. To help you get started with such an approach, we have listed a number of Web addresses in appendix A.

A third way is to scan books and periodicals that cover what churches and other ministries are doing in a variety of contexts. Helpful periodicals include *Leadership Journal, Christianity Today,* and various missions bulletins. Often, pastors of leading-edge churches will write about their ministries (forms). Some examples are Bill Hybel's *Being the Church,* Rick Warren's *The Purpose Driven Church,* and Randy Frazee's *The Connecting Church.*

One form that is clearly emerging as a powerful means of advancing the functions of the church in the twenty-first century is computer technology—specifically the Internet. We're so convinced of its importance to the church that we will devote an entire section of the book (chaps. 6–8) to a discussion of ways to utilize this vital tool.

The Church's Freedom?

The third concept that is important to developing and implementing a church's theology of change is *freedom*. In this section, we'll define freedom, present its biblical basis, and suggest a few restrictions.

What Is the Church's Freedom?

Earlier we defined a ministry's forms as "the temporal, changing, negotiable practices, based on the church's culture and methods, that all churches are free to choose to accomplish their functions." The last part of this definition is key to understanding freedom and its role in the change process. The church isn't free to choose its functions, because they're biblical mandates, but all churches are free to choose the methods they will use to accomplish their functions. For example, the church is not free to decide whether it will worship God. A congregation may largely ignore worship or do it poorly, but that isn't the same as purposely not doing it. The church's freedom applies only to its forms.

When defining a concept, it often helps to talk about what it *isn't* as well as what it *is*. In examining the role of freedom in the change process, I label it as *liberty* and place it on a continuum between two other concepts—*legalism* and *license* (fig. 1).

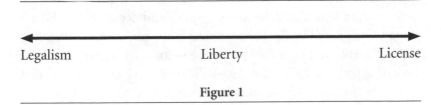

Legalism   Liberty   License

Figure 1

At one extreme is legalism. Legalism drastically limits a church's ability to change. It puts restrictions that aren't found in Scripture on a church's practices (although many people in the church might believe otherwise). To cite an extreme example, I'm aware of a church in Dallas that will not allow couples who use the church's facility for their wedding to play any contemporary music during the ceremony. That's legalism.

The other extreme is license. Freedom or liberty may be confused with license. License removes *any* biblical restrictions on a church's practices. License teaches that the end justifies the means. In other words, as long as we're attempting to reach lost people, anything goes. An example would be tolerating self-centered indulgence and drunkenness at a church event. Paul condemned this very practice in Corinth, where the church celebrated the Lord's Supper in two stages that consolidated eating the bread and drinking the cup at the end of a communal meal. In 1 Corinthians 11:20–21, he writes, "When you come together, it is not the Lord's Supper you eat, for as you eat, each of you goes ahead without waiting for anybody else. One remains hungry, another gets drunk." It's interesting to note that Paul doesn't condemn the Corinthians for serving alcohol at this church event. He condemns them only for getting drunk.

What's the Relationship of Scripture to Freedom?

In two places, James tells us that Scripture promotes freedom. First, in James 1:25, he refers to Scripture as "the perfect law that gives freedom." Associating "the law" with "freedom" seems paradoxical. We tend to view law as limiting freedom. However, God's "perfect law" actually promotes and provides freedom. Individual Christians and their churches will find true freedom when they do what God prescribes for them.

Second, in James 2:12, he writes, "Speak and act as those who are going to be judged by the law that gives freedom, because judgment without mercy will be shown to anyone who has not been merciful." Here he warns his readers that they will be judged by the very law that gives them freedom. His point is that we must not take lightly the freedom that Scripture gives. Liberty is not license. True freedom demands that we speak and act within biblical limits.

Does Freedom Have Restrictions?

Only two restrictions limit our freedom to choose the church's methods or forms. The first is the Bible. Our forms must agree with the Bible. Note that I didn't say that they must be found somewhere in the Bible. A form doesn't have to be found in or practiced in the Bible to be biblical. Instead, the forms must not contradict or disagree with the clear teaching of Scripture. The Bible sets the boundaries, and each church is free under the Holy Spirit to choose its ministry forms within those boundaries.

The second restriction is that the forms we choose must help us to accomplish our biblical functions. If our worship style prohibits godly, spiritual worship, then we must change to a style that promotes proper worship. To practice a particular form simply because we've grown accustomed to it, or because "we've always done it that way," is wrong if it prevents the church from accomplishing the biblical function. If we've always had a church potluck along with the celebration of the Lord's Supper, but the meal detracts from the meaning of Communion, then we must choose another form to accomplish this function.

A quote from Francis Schaeffer provides a fitting conclusion to this chapter on change. He writes, "Not being able, as times change, to change under the Holy Spirit is ugly. The same applies to church polity and practice. In a rapidly changing age like ours, an age of upheaval like ours, to make nonabsolutes absolutes guarantees both isolation and the death of the institutional, organized church."[5]

Questions for Reflection and Discussion

1. Do you or the leaders of your church disagree with any of the major concepts in this chapter? If so, which concepts, and why do you/they disagree with them?
2. Does your church understand that it's okay to change? Why or why not? If not, how has this view affected the church?
3. If your church needs to change, how much time does it have to implement the change before it's too late? What are the chances that it will implement change? Why? What will it take to implement necessary biblical change?
4. Does your church have a theology of change? Why or why not?

If not, is it open to develop such a theology? Why or why not? If it is open, how might you help the church to develop this theology?

5. Identify several biblical functions that your ministry is practicing (e.g., worship and teaching). Next, identify the forms or methods that it uses to practice those functions. Are the methods actually helping your people to experience the intended biblical functions? If not, why not? What are some forms or methods that would help your people to accomplish the functions?

6. Which concept best describes your church's approach to the freedom continuum in figure 1—legalism, liberty, or license? Does freedom exist in your church to discard tired, outdated forms and replace them with fresh, culturally current forms? If not, why not? If not, what could you do about it?

chapter five

Understanding Postmodernism

The term *postmodernism* isn't commonly understood among the members of most churches. If you listen carefully at the next congregational meeting or board meeting, chances are good that you won't hear it mentioned. Of course, the same is true for the grocery store where you shop, the office where you work, and the post office where you mail your letters. However, you will see the concept being discussed and debated in books on theology and philosophy, and you'll hear it discussed on college and seminary campuses. A growing number of people are adopting a postmodernist perspective, and the worldview known as postmodernism is having and will continue to have a profound effect on the United States and the American church. If the church is to make a comeback as a vital cultural force, it will need to do more than target the younger and the current generations and develop a theology of change. It will also need to understand what is invading and capturing the minds, hearts, and souls of young people and what the church can do about it.

Postmodernism isn't simply a philosophical concept tossed around by intellectuals in the ivory towers of some remote university or seminary campuses. Postmodernism is profoundly affecting the thinking of the buster and the bridger generations, not only in our schools, but also inside our churches.

So, what is postmodernism? From where did it come? Who are the postmodernists? What do they believe? And how can Christ's church reach postmodernists effectively and minister to our emerging postmodernist society?

The purpose of this chapter is not to be theologically deep or overly philosophical. Rather, it is to answer these basic questions and give an overview of postmodernism, to familiarize churches and their leaders with this pervasive worldview.

Understanding the Postmodern Context

A good teacher will tell you not to take ideas out of context. If you do, you can make ideas say whatever you want them to. So in order to gain a fair understanding of postmodernism, we must look at it in its context, both historical and philosophical.

The Historical Context

Postmodernism is primarily a product of Western civilization, which traces its roots back to ancient Rome (to 500), and extending up through the Middle Ages (500–1400), the Renaissance (1350–1650), the Reformation (1517–1648), the Enlightenment (1689–1789), Modernism (1789–1989), and culminating in Postmodernism, which began to take shape around 1919 and continues up to the present. Each phase in the development of Western civilization contributed in some way to postmodernism, but modernism has had the greatest and most direct impact.

Postmodernism is a reaction to the modernist worldview and stands in stark contrast to modernism in many ways (table 1). The age of modernism corresponds historically with the Industrial Revolution, whereas postmodernism has accelerated through the Information Revolution with information technology leading the way. Under modernism, America experienced a deep sense of nationalism. Postmodernism and the Internet, however, have moved younger Americans toward a greater sense of globalism. Modernism bought heavily into Descartes' concept of man's autonomous self, whereas postmodernism emphasizes community. Each view holds to a different authority. Modernism's authority is reason; postmodernism's authority is experience. Modernism has an optimistic view of life; postmodernism began with a pessimistic view that seems to be shifting back toward optimism.

THE MODERNIST/POSTMODERNIST CLASH

Modernism	Postmodernism
Industrial Revolution	Information Revolution
Nationalism	Globalism
Autonomous self	Authentic community
Authority: reason (Descartes)	Authority: experience
Optimism	Pessimism
Man is good	Man is bad
Natural world	Supernatural world
Skeptical	Spiritual
Didactic	Narrative
Scientists, educators	Artists, poets
Noncontradiction	Contradiction
Discover truth (scientific method)	Create truth
Metanarrative	Metanarratives

Table 1

Other differences exist as well. Modernism assumes that man is basically good; postmodernism assumes that man is essentially bad. Modernism presupposes a natural world in which nothing exists outside of nature; postmodernism views the world supernaturally and believes in a world outside of nature. Modernists are skeptical about spiritual things; postmodernists believe in and are deeply interested in spiritual things, but not necessarily the spiritual things of the Bible. Modernists prefer a logical, didactic approach to literature such as the Bible; postmodernists love stories and therefore prefer biblical narrative. In fact, postmodernists view reality as a system of overlapping narratives, and they not only want to hear your story but also to tell you theirs. The modernists' heroes are the scientists and the educators; the postmodernists' heroes are the poets and the artists, those who communicate creatively. Modernists believe that truth is out there somewhere and that we can discover it through the scientific method; postmodernists believe that truth is within us (our truth is what is true to us), and thus we create our own truth. Modernists believe in non-contradiction (i.e., that ideas shouldn't contradict each other); postmodernists have no problems with contradictions (seeing them as simply overlapping narratives). Finally, modernists believe that there's one overarching metanarrative (a story or truth into which all truth fits); postmodernists believe in many metanarratives or many different "true truths."

The Philosophical Context

The philosophical context of Western civilization is the various worldviews that have bridged and affected these civilizations. I define a dominant worldview as a set of beliefs about the most important issues in life that help a significant number of people, such as an entire civilization, make sense of their world. A dominant worldview includes beliefs about such concepts as God, the world, truth, reality, morality, and humanity.

Western civilization has experienced four dominant worldviews (table 2), and each was generally a reaction to its predecessor. Theism was the dominant Western worldview from the Middle Ages up to the end of the seventeenth century. Deism had a limited impact that affected Western culture from the late seventeenth through the eighteenth centuries. Modernism or philosophical naturalism prevailed beginning in the eighteenth century up through 1989 (the fall of the Berlin Wall) and is still the dominant worldview in the West. Postmodernism or philosophical supernaturalism[1] most likely began in 1919 with Arthur Eddington's expedition that established Einstein's Theory of Relativity. And postmodernism is becoming a dominant worldview in America.[2]

WESTERN WORLDVIEWS
Theism
Deism
Modernism (Naturalism)
Postmodernism (Supernaturalism)
Table 2

As a worldview, modernism seems to have fallen on hard times. It hasn't passed the test of experience. Horrified by such events as the Holocaust and terrified by crime and the threat of nuclear war, postmodernists have observed correctly that science hasn't solved all of the world's problems as promised and that humans are evil far beyond what a good education can repair. And the modernist emphasis on rational thought that purportedly routed the Bible and its miracles has left them cold.

Although modernism is still strong in America even among the younger generations, postmodernism seems gradually to be capturing the allegiance of many younger Americans. Postmodern advocates argue that no one universal story (metanarrative) or universal truth can hold for all time because truth isn't objective, it's subjective, depending on who is speaking and who is listening. Instead, many truths (metanarratives) exist because truth is relative to various individuals, their cultures, and their individual circumstances. Truth for one person isn't automatically truth for another person, contrary to the modernist perspective.

Postmodernists have also challenged and deconstructed literature, history, and even religion, meaning that they reject everything that people have believed about their stories, heroes, and even God.

"Diversity" and "tolerance" are in fashion, whereas traditional authority and moral pronouncements are out.

Not everyone agrees, however, that postmodernism is now the reigning worldview. Some people believe that the postmodernist party is already over. You can only thumb your nose at the rules for so long; ultimately people want rules by which to live. Critics argue that modernism was about construction whereas postmodernism is all about deconstruction, and no worldview can survive such a negative, cynical approach to life that tears down without reconstructing. For example, Sally Morgenthaler writes, "Postmodernism is no foundation for a fulfilled, rewarding life. Postmodernism is a response to something, but it is not a solution in and of itself. It is a commentary, not a text, and people, everybody, needs a text to live by. They need a narrative to live within which can give their lives meaning."[3]

Although all of this has yet to play out, we've already noted in chapter 4 that the bridger generation is typically much more optimistic than the buster generation, a generation that reacted strongly (and negatively) to the older, optimistic boomer generation. Perhaps postmodernism as a worldview is waning; however, it has made such an impact on American life and Christianity that the church must not take it lightly. Worldviews die a slow death. Thus it's doubtful that any church that ignores postmodernism will be effective at reaching busters and bridgers.

Postmodernist Pegs

Because postmodernism is a worldview, anyone—regardless of age or generation—can be a postmodernist. All one has to do is embrace a postmodernist perspective in how he or she understands and relates to the world. However, few boomers, and even fewer builders, have adopted postmodernism, because they have been so completely immersed in modernism. Although elements of postmodernism have been around since 1919, it did not begin to exert itself fully until the second half of the twentieth century. Consequently, postmodernism is more characteristic of the younger generations such as the busters and bridgers. However, we must be careful not to blanket these two generations with a postmodernist label. Not all busters and bridgers are postmodernists. As we've discovered, modernism is still alive and well in the lives of America's youth.

What is important to grasp, however, is the spiritual state of these two younger generations. Whether they're modern or postmodern thinkers, they're not doing well spiritually. This is a serious concern when you consider that they're the two predominant generations in America and now outnumber the boomers and builders combined. George Barna has warned that two-thirds of the younger generations shun all organized religion. And Thom Rainer has warned that only 4 percent of the bridgers understand the gospel and have accepted Christ, even if they are churched. Clearly this is the church's challenge in the twenty-first century, to continue to pursue these new generations while continuing to reach out to builders and boomers.

What Postmodernists Believe

As we examine briefly what postmodernists believe, we must remember that postmodernism is a mind-set that helps them to understand and relate to the world. What they believe affects how they think and react when they consider the claims of Christ or any other religion or spiritual movement (e.g., Islam, New Age). We'll look briefly at nine tenets, or postmodern pegs, on which most postmodernists would hang their caps.

There Is No Absolute Truth

Postmodernists believe that truth is relative. What is true in one situation or culture isn't necessarily true in another setting or culture. Therefore, Christ must be wrong when He claims in John 14:6 that He is the way, the truth, and the life, and that no one can come to the Father except through Him. The obvious problem is that what Jesus said is an absolute and absolutes are not allowed. Of course, the view that there are no absolutes is itself an absolute statement that contradicts and disproves the postmodernists' own premise. The problem, however, is that postmodernists reject the law of noncontradiction. Thus they have no problem holding mutually contradictory positions.

Reality Is in the Mind of the Beholder

Postmodernists believe that reality is what is real to them or to me or you; hence, reality is in the mind of the beholder. What is real to me might not be real to you—but that's okay. Neither of us is wrong; actually, we can both be right—for ourselves. Christianity might be real to me but not to you. However, as a Christian, I would be wrong to push my beliefs on you.

Intuition and Feelings Are Okay

Intuition and feelings are valid means to discover reality. Reason and logic no longer reign supreme. Humanity is basically bad, and that affects our capacity to reason. Consequently, reason is no more valid than one's feelings or intuition as a means for interpreting reality. It was okay for Jesus to resort to reason when He encountered doubting Thomas in John 20:24–29 and asked him to touch the nail marks in His hands and the wound in His side. However, from a postmodernist perspective, to appeal to Thomas's intuition and feelings about what had happened would have been just as valid an approach.

Science and Education Prove Nothing

Science, education, history, and other logic-based disciplines no longer have a corner on the market of truth, because these disciplines attempt to discover truth using primarily the scientific method. We, however, are able to create our own truths, because truth is whatever you or I decide it is. Consequently, Christ was wrong when in John 8:31–32 He said that His objective, propositional teaching was key to the Jews' knowing truth.

Culture Molds Our Minds

Culture largely affects what people think and do. It has so invaded and molded their thinking that they're unable to think independently apart from their culture; therefore, truth is relative to one's culture. This means that all lifestyles, religions, and worldviews are culture-based; therefore, no one view is more valid than any other view—they simply differ based on cultural concepts. Thus, Christians have no business judging other cultures, and Christian missionaries have no business going to other cultures to persuade them to adopt the "objective truths" of Christian culture. However, if we follow this line of reasoning, we would have to conclude that Hitler must have been right (within his own cultural understanding), and racism in America is okay, too, because truth is relative to one's culture.

The Glass Is Half Empty

Postmodernists are pessimists. Their glass is half empty. They believe that we must view the future with pessimism and cynicism because we're digressing, not progressing, as a society. Disciplines such as science and education have failed to deliver on their promises—to conquer diseases and to educate people—and thus have failed to make this world a better place. We aren't any better off today than we were in the past. For example, we still have as many criminals as we did in the past. The only difference is that they're healthier and better educated now. As is the case with some of the other tenets of postmodernism, there is some truth here. Modernism hasn't delivered on its promises because it has no power to change sinners into saints. Only the Holy Spirit can accomplish this feat through the absolute, objective truth of the gospel.

Tolerance and Acceptance Rule

We must never criticize or seek to correct other people's views or moral choices; rather, we should treat them with tolerance and acceptance. To do otherwise is to commit the sin of intolerance. The terms *tolerance* and *acceptance* are postmodern buzzwords that appear repeatedly in their writings. In short, it's inappropriate to tell someone else that they're wrong. To hold that one's beliefs are true not only for themselves but also for others is bigoted and narrow-minded. The problem for postmodernists, however, is that they take this position only so far. They don't show tolerance or acceptance for views—such as Christianity—that differ with their own.

Justice for the Marginalized

We must do justice to the claims of the marginalized—those who historically have not been heard, such as women, gays, lesbians, non-Northern Europeans, and others. We must listen to these people. Their claims and ideas deserve the same kind of historical and philosophical attention that we give to those of mainstream America. Again, much here is true. However, just because a marginalized people haven't been heard or given due attention doesn't mean that what they're saying is true.

Metanarratives Are Essentially Power Plays

At the heart of every truth claim is a story, or metanarrative (absolute truth), that enhances one group but marginalizes another. Consequently, what is really taking place in America is an attempt by one group to impose its metanarrative on another group. This, in effect, is a philosophical or political power play to subjugate others—most often the marginalized—in the guise of absolute truth.

Postmodern Players

In football, when a team is performing poorly, the coach will do practically anything at halftime to motivate his team. He might jump up on a bench and shout, "Okay, who wants to win this game? Who are my players?" The church has also experienced a difficult first half, and it, too, needs to know who wants to win this game. Who'll be its players?

We have one final goal for this chapter. We must probe what kind of church Christ will use to reach the postmodern world. I predict that successful churches will come in all shapes, sizes, and colors, because it takes a diverse church to reach a diverse society. However, I believe that along with other general functions—such as people mobilization, leadership development, and other activities—the church must accomplish the following tasks in particular.

A Church That Teaches and Lives the Bible

In order to capture the postmodernists' attention, the church must teach and live the Bible. Regardless of the generation, there can be no substitute for the communication of God's Word. However, it's imperative that pastors teach and preach from the narrative portions (such as the Gospels, Acts, and much of the Old Testament) as well as from the Epistles. The tendency in the modern context is to teach more from the didactic portions (such as the New Testament epistles) because of the prevailing modernist emphasis on reason and logic. However, postmodernists love narrative and also want God's truth in the context of a story (metanarrative), and that fits very well with the biblical narrative genre. After all, the gospel is a metanarrative. This doesn't mean, of course, that the church avoids didactic literature or any of the other genres found in the Bible. God has chosen a rich diversity of genres in which to record His Word.

Postmodernists are looking for Christians who *live* the Bible as well as listen to it or read it. In other words, Christians must "walk their talk" or sit down and be quiet. This is what some people refer to as incarnational Christianity. Postmodernists aren't interested in the typical apologetics that were persuasive with the modern generations. *Evidence That Demands a Verdict* doesn't cut it with them. Incarnational Christians are the primary Bible that lost, unchurched postmodernists will read. If they don't see the reality of Christ displayed there, in the lives of Christians, they won't bother opening a leatherbound Bible. Far too many young people have joined the ranks of the unchurched because they've attended churches where the older, established generations have become complacent doing church a particular way. This well-meaning establishment is reluctant or afraid to change the ways in which they've always done things because they might lose control. The tragedy is that many of these Christians have sat under good Bible teaching for thirty or forty years, but they've not applied much of it to their lives. The result is that they've run off and marginalized their young people.

A Church That Is Proactive in Evangelism

I'm somewhat troubled by a new church in Dallas that seeks to minister to lost postmodernists. The *Dallas Morning News* featured a story about this church and quoted the pastor as saying that "conversion is downplayed in favor of community." In light of the New Testament teaching in general and the Great Commission in particular, this statement alarms me. Although I'm for new paradigm churches, those churches must function biblically. Scripture provides the final say about how we do church, what we can and can't do. As we saw in chapter 4, although the Bible gives us much freedom in the forms that our churches take, it does require certain functions. Community is important, but not at the expense of conversion. Perhaps that pastor's idea is that authentic community enhances conversion, but he doesn't say that.

The church that reaches postmodernists must be proactive and "play up," not downplay, the gospel and the importance of conversion. The obvious reason is that conversion makes the difference between heaven and hell and whether one exists in the kingdom of light or the kingdom of darkness. And it's the gospel that leads to conversion.

Although the Bible is about more than just the gospel, the gospel is certainly central, and the Bible has a lot to say about it. Postmodernists need to know that the gospel is a metanarrative (story) that doesn't oppress or marginalize people. In fact, the gospel is *the* metanarrative that tells the truth, the story of how Jesus was "marginalized" on behalf of all who are the marginalized. (Whether poor or oppressed, we've all been marginalized by the ravages of sin.) Although the use of the term *marginalized* doesn't begin to capture what the Savior experienced on the cross, it does communicate in a way that is consistent with a postmodernist worldview—and thinking postmodernists will recognize this.

The church of the twenty-first century must be missional. And the Savior made it clear in Mark 16:15 and Matthew 28:19–20 that his church's mission includes the conversion of lost people and the making of disciples. We discussed in chapter 2 that the American church is not only struggling in evangelism but is also not winning the younger generations—especially the bridgers—to faith in Christ. America has become a mission field. Consequently, a missionary mind-set that focuses on conversion must be near the top of the "to-do list" for any church that seeks to reach postmodernists.

A Church That's Creative in Worship

When we worship, we attribute extreme worth to our God, who is a most creative God. Because those with a postmodern mind-set tend to be culturally creative, churches that seek to reach postmodernists will attribute extreme worth to a creative God in creative ways. For example, the church must find creative ways to include the use of such media as painting, music, film, film clips, poetry, drama, dance, and other creative art forms. In its creativeness, the church will pursue new, contemporary worship forms, revive historic worship forms, and combine the old with the new.

Creative Christians won't be content to limit themselves only to traditional forms of worship. They'll constantly be exploring new and different ways to worship God. They might include a corporate reading, painting, creative dance, film clips that highlight some aspect of the sermon, and other forms that haven't even been thought of yet. (Some churches are already using creative dance and film clips in their worship.) They'll not be content with old music forms alone. This is too confining of worship. They will constantly be writing new music to aid the church in expressing the wonders of our marvelous God.

At the same time, some new paradigm churches have returned, and will continue to return, to worship forms of the past. Churches that are currently reaching out to busters often depend heavily on sixth-century liturgy, monastic images, and recitation of a creed or response to a catechism as part of their worship. These activities often take place in a setting with a plethora of candles, and Communion is served every week.

Some churches that reach postmodernists will merge the old with the new. They might mix the liturgy, the Nicene Creed, and a corporate reading with Christian alternative rock. They might blend the neoclassical with a touch of Celtic. They could combine a little bit of Christian rock, Christian jazz, or Christian rap with ancient texts and prayers.

As occurred in the past, these churches will worship in a variety of locations. They'll use such contexts as an inner city storefront, a nightclub, a fitness center, or a facility that belongs to an older church. Regardless of the form or the location, the object will be to divert the worshippers' attention away from the particular form or location to focus on our awesome God.

A Church That Is Authentic

A characteristic of postmodernists is their strong desire for authenticity. The church that reaches postmodernists will pursue authenticity. This isn't exactly new. The boomer generation also appreciates churches that practice authenticity.

About ten years ago, I worked as a consultant with a church whose board consisted of boomers and builders. My assignment was to assist and advise them in their pursuit of a new pastor. While we were discussing the characteristics of a good pastor for their church, one of the builder members strongly expressed that he wanted a pastor who didn't talk about his shortcomings and failures from the pulpit. He asked, "How can we follow a pastor who doesn't have it all together?"

Before he could finish, one of the boomer members interrupted him angrily and stated, "That's exactly what we need, a pastor who's willing to admit publicly that he doesn't have it all together!" That's authenticity.

Nothing has changed with the younger generations. The problem is that most of them struggle to define authenticity. Mark Driscoll writes, "Authenticity is when your inside matches your outside, one person said. It is two parts integrity and one part self-disclosure. It is not soul-letting without a tourniquet, but a willingness to share from one's faith experience for the benefit of others is required."[4] Driscoll is correct. Authenticity includes the willingness to disclose publicly your shortcomings as well as your successes. Some young people would say that it's "being real."

The twenty-first-century church can display authenticity in a number of contexts. One must be the pulpit. Preaching pastors must have the freedom to verbalize their shortcomings and vulnerabilities. There must be a willingness to share from their faith experience that includes defeats as well as victories. Most congregations know that pastors are frail human beings, but they do need to hear them admit it from time to time. Even more important, many congregants consider themselves pilgrims who want to learn from pilgrim pastors who are a little farther along in their spiritual journeys and have bled some along the way.

The church that pursues authenticity would also be wise to have an active small-group ministry. Authenticity is developed and nurtured in the context of community. *Community,* as I'm using the term here, means a gathering of believers. Most Christians desire to build deep relationships with a small group of other, like-minded believers. This is especially a characteristic of and most important to the busters and the bridgers. However, this kind of community demands authenticity. People fellowship and relate best with one another when they can talk about their shortcomings and struggles with others who will listen and give comfort.

A Church That Values Community

Some of the more seeker-oriented boomer churches value anonymity, because they realized that many seekers from the builder and boomer generations preferred to be left alone to consider the claims of Christ without having to stand and introduce themselves or interact with the people sitting near them. So these churches created a style of service where these people could come and participate at their own discretion.

Busters and bridgers might prefer anonymity when they first make contact with a church. However, they are ultimately more interested in being part of a community of believers. Busters and bridgers are two generations that highly value community, and the term often punctuates their conversations about the ideal church.

The type of community they desire most is biblical community, which is what occurs when believers practice the "one another" passages that are sprinkled throughout the New Testament. These passages exhort Christians to pray for one another, encourage one another, confront one another, care for one another, and engage in numerous other "one another" ministries. At the core of biblical community is a commitment to share who they are and relate at length and in depth with one another. Acts 2:42–47 and Acts 4:32–35 provide us with a first-century snapshot of biblical community. It includes such events as spending time together, sharing and holding possessions in common, providing for one another's needs, and other ministries. For today's young person, getting to know God often involves getting to know the people of God first. And community is the way they can get to know the people of God best.

The church that reaches postmodernists in the twenty-first century will develop new structures that encourage community. Many churches have already developed small-group ministries with the intent to cultivate biblical community. As we train church planters, we ask them, "Will your future churches be faith communities *with* small groups, or a community *of* small groups?" In other words, "Will your ministries *include* small groups, or will your ministries *consist* primarily of small groups?" Churches with small groups programs *include* community, but churches of small groups *are* community.

A Church That Uses Technology

Over the last twenty years or so, America has experienced a technological explosion. Technology that wasn't around five to ten years ago is now part of our everyday lives. It's common to see people on the street with a cell phone mounted on their hip or plastered to their ear. Churches that reach postmodernists won't hesitate to use technology in their ministry.

The problem up till now is that the church has been hesitant at best to incorporate technology. Lyle Schaller, who is of the builder generation, tells how difficult it was for the church to embrace the telephone when it first became available. And he shares humorously how some people greeted the church's move to adopt indoor plumbing with the following words: "We're not going to do that in the house of God are we?" One wonders how long it took the church to adopt the printing press when it first became available in the middle of the fourteenth century. In order to reach postmodernists effectively, the church must look at the available technology and ask how it can be used creatively for the cause of Christ.

Our particular concern in this book is the use of the Internet and related technology to advance the mission of the church. If, as I mentioned earlier, as many as three out of four Americans go online, the Internet has clearly become a mainstream activity that should be utilized by the church. A report by the Pew Internet and American Life Project indicates that, in 2001, 25 percent of people used the Internet for religious purposes (up from 21 percent in 2000) an increase that equates to nineteen or twenty million people. The report states, "For comparison's sake, it is interesting to note that more people have gotten religious or spiritual information online than have gambled online, used Web auction sites, traded stocks online, placed phone calls on the Internet, done online banking, or used Internet-based dating services."[5]

We believe that Americans are just beginning to warm to the idea of using the Internet for religious purposes. Therefore, a primary challenge for the church early in the twenty-first century will be to harness the Internet and use it powerfully for the cause of Christ. And it's to this challenge that we address the rest of this work.

Questions for Reflection and Discussion

1. Have you ever heard the term *postmodernism* used around your church? If yes, when and by whom? If not, why not?
2. Would the people in your church be able to define post-modernism? Why or why not?
3. Name some of the differences between postmodernism and modernism.
4. How has postmodernism affected Christ's church? Has it affected your church? If so, how?
5. Does your church have any of the forms of the kind of church that will reach postmodernists? If yes, which ones? If not, why not?
6. How might your church become one that reaches post-modernists? What do you believe the chances are of this happening? If your answer is that the chances aren't good, what will you do about it?

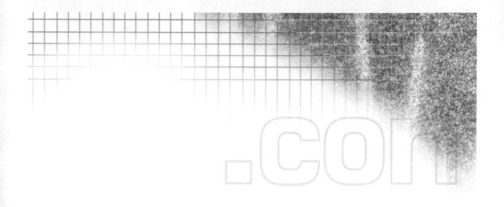

part three

The Method:
eMinistry in the
Twenty-First Century

chapter six

The Importance
of the Internet

What effect has the Internet had on the nation? So far, it has been phenomenal. Almost three-fourths of Americans go online, for reasons that include e-mailing, instant messaging, Web browsing, shopping, news, and other options.

Second, and more important, what effect has the Internet had on Americans' spiritual lives? A recent Barna Report indicates that within this decade, as many as fifty million people might rely solely on the Internet to provide all of their faith-based experiences. However, Barna explains that Americans are only just beginning to warm to the cyberfaith idea. He predicts that as many as two-thirds of Americans will engage regularly in Net-based religious pursuits in this decade. This activity will include virtually every dimension of the faith community such as missions, evangelism, online devotionals, theological chats, streaming video sermons, online meetings and services, broadcasts to those who are homebound, theological training, and many other events.[1]

Recently, I chatted with a missionary friend who said that his mission was relying heavily on the Internet to reach Muslims. The reason is that a good Muslim can't be seen spending time with a missionary or even a Christian. Any hint of openness to Christianity could earn him a one-way ticket back to his home country. However, a Muslim can now go online in the privacy of his own home to a Web site that presents the truth about Christianity and addresses all of the standard Muslim objections.

Because predicting the future of technology is nearly impossible—let alone predicting the future of its use in the church—we will not attempt to foresee the face of technology ten, twenty, or fifty years from now. Undoubtedly, it will look very different than it does today. However, we can explore the use of current Internet technology in bringing unbelievers to Christ and believers closer together.

In earlier chapters, we saw evidence that the typical church is lagging twenty to thirty years behind the culture, in terms of adapting its forms to meet the needs of a changing society. This is certainly true when it comes to the rapid changes in technology that we see today. Yet, with church attendance in decline—along with a decline in the number of born-again Christians—the body of Christ can no longer afford not to pursue cultural relevance. Instead, we must seize the day and use the tools that God has given us to fulfill the Great Commission.

One such tool is the Internet. Increasingly, people are using the Internet to check churches before they visit. They will attend a church whose Web site meets their needs but often will ignore a church with a poor site. To understand and begin to use this tool effectively, we must first realize the impact and importance of this new medium. In the *New Republic,* Esther Dyson writes, "Because it is such a powerful tool, it is incumbent upon people who want to change the world for the better to learn how to use it."[2] Failing to do so means that we will not only risk cultural irrelevancy but we'll also miss running the ultimate race of all—the race for the future of the church.

What Has Been the Impact of the Internet?

This fact is amazing considering that just ten years ago the Internet had little impact on our daily lives.

For the average individual going through his or her day, it is impossible not to come face-to-face with new technology. Whether receiving e-mail from coworkers and friends or balancing a checkbook through an online bank account, technology is all around us, and much of it is Internet related. In their annual Internet study, researchers at UCLA report, "The Internet is now a mainstream activity in American life that continues to spread among people across all age groups, education levels, and incomes. The majority of Americans have e-mail, use online technology, and buy online, and new and experienced users alike view the Internet as a key source of information."[3]

YEARS TO REACH 30% OF HOMES

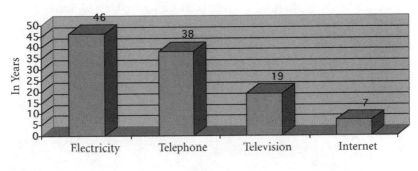

Figure 1

How far does this impact reach? In a 1997 *Newsweek* article, Steven Levy reported, "The world is on the cusp of an economic and cultural shift as dramatic as that of the Industrial Revolution."[4] And the numbers back him up. As of September 2002, there were 606 million Internet users worldwide and 183 million in North America alone.[5] This number translates into 71.1 percent of Americans, up from 66.9 percent in 2000. In addition, the typical Internet user is online an average of 11.1 hours per week.[6] Considering these numbers and the staggering three billion Web pages posted on the World Wide Web, no wonder Internet use continues to grow at an unbelievable pace despite current economic and social troubles worldwide.

This rapid rate of growth is unlike any other technology in history. Consider the following statistics. After the invention of electricity, it took forty-six years for 30 percent of American homes to become wired. Thirty-eight years passed before the telephone reached 30 percent of homes. Television took only half that time, but the Internet achieved the same mark in only seven years! (See fig. 1.)

And there's more. The UCLA report found that in the United States, 55,000 new users log on each day, 2,289 each hour, and 38 each minute. In 1997, nineteen million Americans went online, and the number tripled in 1998. These ranks grew to include one hundred million people in 1999, and research indicates that the number will be two hundred million by the end of 2003 (fig. 2). And let's not forget about e-mail and the Web. Every twenty-four hours, the World Wide Web increases by more than 3.2 million pages, and the United States Postal Service estimates that more than four trillion e-mail messages are delivered each year.[7]

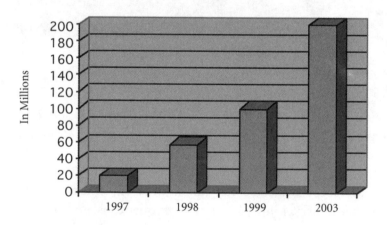

INTERNET GROWTH 1997–2003

Figure 2

Most telling of all, though, is how pervasive the Internet has become. More and more people are using it and watching less TV. Individuals are forming social circles online, and parents are urging children to use the Internet for schoolwork. Employers are providing employees with an Internet connection, and many people simply work at home by telecommuting. Internet users now average nearly eleven hours online per week browsing, shopping, and communicating with friends via instant messaging. And many of us spend a good part of our workday gathering information on the Internet for various projects. Overall, our lives are becoming rich with the information and communication abilities provided by the Internet.

This communication power and information gathering is a primary reason for the Internet's pervasiveness in our culture. We are now able to keep in touch more regularly with friends and family members and become better established in social groups. With the ability to research anything, anytime online, work is made easier and is less constrained. We can pursue hobbies, learn about the world, and become more informed citizens, all of which are high priorities with America's youth.

Indeed, Generations X and Y have quickly embraced this new technology. More than 81 percent of those ages twelve to seventeen are online,[8] and thirteen million of them use instant messaging. Schools propel Internet use upward, as most public schools make Internet access available to students. Almost 100 percent of college graduates have online access and nine out of ten of them send and receive e-mail every day.[9] This technology is as entrenched with the young as the telephone is with their elders.

The Internet's growth and pervasiveness points toward the important role that it will play in tomorrow's church. Let's take a further look at the social and spiritual implications of this remarkable technology.

IN-DEPTH Q AND A—THEOOZE

Site: www.theooze.com

Webmaster: Spencer Burke

TheOoze is a new kind of online community focused on helping believers grow in their relationship with God, connect with one another, and influence their world by providing a destination that postmodernists can taste, touch, see, smell, and hear.

> Why was the Web site built? What are the goals of the site?

TheOoze came online in 1999 as a result of our efforts to find reasonable ways to make connections within the Christian community. Our main goal is to provide a place that facilitates real, honest, and authentic communication, all in a powerful way.

One way of viewing our site is to understand that we are trying to find the Calvins of today's world. The Internet provides a great place to listen to and talk with one another; accordingly, TheOoze creates a safe place for Christians to share with one another.

We have many goals for our site, including a creative think-tank called "TheOoze Tank." "Districts" provide a way for people to gather not by denomination or age, but by location. Also, "Guilds" provide another way for people to get together and to talk about different subjects such as film, church planting, and more. This group is a more focused group that can share and learn from each other.

> Where did the inspiration for the site come from?

I have more than twenty years of ministry experience, including involvement in youth ministries. I have watched carefully the way that religious ministry and the church have evolved over the past twenty years. And TheOoze developed naturally from this experience.

Over the years, I have observed that many people think that they must drop the way they naturally pray. They believe that losing their own, unique language is a more "Christian" approach to their faith. But at TheOoze we won't disenfranchise anyone who disagrees with us. Indeed, the Internet allows us to tell others that the way you've packaged Christianity in the past might not be the complete truth. TheOoze allows us to ask how we might have changed the gospel and how we can unlock its true nature. This simply gets back to the essence of the gospel. Regardless, passion always finds a way to use the most aggressive tools.

> Who is your target audience? Do they match your typical visitor?

Our typical visitor and target audience are postmodern Americans ages eighteen to thirty-five who are willing to ask themselves and others deep questions. Often, their approach to Christianity is radically different than those of Christians in the past. Instead of spam evangelism, our members enter our message boards or chat rooms without rules, willing to ask and discuss anything.

> What kind of response are you receiving?

Well, we are not about getting a certain number of hits or memberships. As a matter of fact, we haven't spent any money on advertising. Our growth has been strictly by word of mouth. That said, the site has grown dramatically month by month, and response has been outrageous.

But we have had many negative reactions to our ministry. Any time someone steps out of the norm, other people get concerned or grow wary. Yet, this does not concern or bother most people who are involved with the site. Fortunately, our site is a different animal that only God controls.

> What are the most popular sections/features of the site?

The most popular section of the site is definitely the Church Locator. People are always trying to find a church in their area that does things differently. Our message boards and chat rooms—places that facilitate discussion—are very popular as well.

> Share one success story that has come from your Internet ministry.

I always enjoy the hundreds of e-mails I get that say, "Thank you." It shows that TheOoze has been a worthwhile effort, even if it is just helping others find people similar to themselves.

> What role do you think the Internet will play in the future of the church?

It is important because of its ability to create and support Christian communities. With online publishing, learning, and music, the Internet is a new channel of distribution. But remember that the Internet is only a tool to complement the myriad ministry options that we have today.

> In the future, what would you like to see happen with the church on the Internet?

Most Christian Web sites are terrible because they answer only the "how" questions that revolve around building a Web site. But they must also take the time to tackle the "why" questions. In other words, "Why are we doing this?" This is crucial not only to a single Web site but also to the role that the Internet will play in the future of our church.

> What suggestions do you have for those who want to build a ministry-based site?

An overall principle is that you allow people to play on your site. Permit as much dynamic creation and as many dynamic controls as possible, and the site will take on a life of its own. This can be as simple as putting up a message board, but I would stay away from chat rooms because they are so difficult to maintain.

I also encourage people to take their Web sites one step at a time. Every tragic Web story that I hear includes the over-capitalization of a site. The only way TheOoze has survived to this point is by keeping it simple and taking everything one day at a time. A Web site is a huge endeavor that requires an enormous vision. If you are going to build one, ensure that you are familiar with the culture and values of the Internet. You don't want to bring the old world into the new.

Why Is the Internet Important?

As we have seen, the Internet is having a massive effect on our surroundings. Its impressive rate of growth and adoption make it a driving force in our society. And this influence is changing both the world and the people living within it. It is a twofold change that is having a social impact on the world and a spiritual impact on the church.

These two seemingly disparate views will provide us with a solid understanding of the Internet's importance on both a macro scale (the world) and a micro scale (the church). Then, and only then, can we truly begin to understand what role the Internet has in ministering to the human race.

The Internet Has a Social Impact

One reason for the great influence of the Internet is the grassroots, communal nature of the technology. The Internet has more communication ability than all other media combined; e-mail is helping bring those who are apart closer together; and the Web, with its ability to help individuals find information and each other, is making the globe a smaller place.

Because the Internet is used primarily at home rather than at work, people spend more time using it for socializing and meeting new friends. Research has found that users spend 2.3 hours more per week online at home than at any other place.[10] But they are not going online primarily for entertainment, as many people would lead us to believe, they're going online for e-mail and other communication purposes. Jeffrey Cole of UCLA reports, "More than 77 percent of e-mail users agree or strongly agree that e-mail allows them to communicate with people they could not normally talk to as often."[11] Users also report an astounding average of twenty-one friends made online. The same study also brings to light that Internet users spend more time socializing with friends than do those who are not connected.

The Internet strongly affects the family, but not in the dire ways we might expect. One statistic shows that 88.8 percent of Internet users report spending as much or more time with each other since becoming connected, and more than 80 percent say their communication has improved.[12] With the decline in family relationships and family values evident throughout our society, these statistics are astonishing. We would be wise to welcome aid to strengthen our families and communities.

The Internet has also brought other unexpected benefits. TV viewing is down, parents report that their children's grades are rising, and some reports indicate a slightly higher level of life satisfaction among those who are connected. Does this seem too good to be true? Not among Internet users. A solid 62 percent think that the world has become a better place because of communication technology such as the Internet.[13]

But how does all this fit into what Christ established as our main goal to fulfill here on earth—the Great Commission? The answer lies not only in the social impact of the Internet but in its spiritual impact as well. Here is where the Church must connect to bring more and more individuals to Christ.

How Can the Internet Have a Spiritual Impact?

Every day, an increasing number of individuals use the Internet to investigate spiritual matters. Research indicates that more people use the Internet to search for religious information than for such activities as online auctions or banking. More than three million individuals go online every day looking for spiritual content, and 25 percent of Internet users have done so.[14] Many people include the Internet as a major part of their lives, turning to e-mail and the Web several times a week for needed information. The data also indicate that the online population can't get enough spiritual fulfillment and are starved in their spiritual needs.

The Internet provides easier access to religious information and materials than is available offline. Almost half the respondents in recent surveys said that this increased availability and other aspects of the Internet have steadily improved their spiritual lives, and they are finding others with whom they can share their beliefs more easily online. Being able to speak freely with others about how they feel, even just through e-mail or chat rooms, makes believers more confident in their faith.

With all of the religious groups around today, it would be easy to view these people as just part of a diverse mix of unrelated religions. Don't be fooled. Christians represent a major portion of those who go online (fig. 3). Patrick Dixon, an Internet researcher, found that three times as many Web sites are devoted to Christianity than any other major world religion, and that the Net contains more than six million references to Christianity.

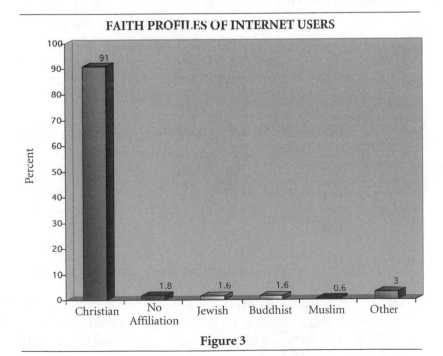

FAITH PROFILES OF INTERNET USERS

Figure 3

A recent Barna study also supports this view. According to Barna's research, born-again Christians adopt technology at the same rate as non-Christians, and they are every bit as likely to use the Internet as other groups.[15] Another study conducted in Britain found that Internet users are 50 percent more likely to attend church each week than are nonusers.[16] The theory that Christians are shying away from these new technologies is simply not substantiated by the evidence.

Individual Christians are not the only ones benefiting from the Internet. Churches are finding a renewed identity and passion for Christ through modern communications technology. The Pew Internet and American Life Project found that 81 percent of the churches surveyed reported that e-mail use by church clergy, staff, and members has helped the spiritual life of the congregation. And 91 percent reported that e-mail has placed them in greater communication with their fellow congregants.

> By creating better ties within a preexisting community, by creating a Web presence, and by facilitating discussions that can be difficult to hold in other settings, congregations tightened bonds with their groups, reestablished connections with former members, and in some cases, expanded their missions on a global scale.[17]

Clearly, with the Internet, we are seeing a true revolution in the church and the world. But we must be clear about one issue. Christ has laid the foundation for a Church-based Internet revolution, and we must continue to look to Him for guidance in using the Internet as a tool to reach modern society. This singular truth is the basis for all that is to follow.

The Internet: An Essential Tool for the Church's Survival

Let's face it, when you think of the Internet and the church, you don't think of a pulpit and pews. Our churches have never done a good job of keeping up with emerging technology. For example, with the printing press, Martin Luther published more works during his life than the entire Roman Catholic Church published during the same period of time. Many churches didn't install basic utilities such as plumbing and electricity until years after they were widely available. Even the telephone is still considered taboo among some of the more legalistic churches today.

There seems to have always been a stigma surrounding technology in the church. Most people feel uncomfortable with it. It's hard to say where and when this stigma originated, but it's fair to say that the whole church must overcome this fear quickly if we are to continue to reach people for Christ.

"The Internet has much to offer the church," says Andrew Careaga, "and it's time to integrate the positive aspects of Net technology and culture into our Christ-centered traditions and move toward creating a growing, thriving, renewed vision of true church within our congregations."[18]

It is impossible to predict the future of the Internet, but it is clearly not just a fleeting blip on the radar—here today, gone tomorrow. Integrating this technology into our evangelism, missions, and lifestyle is now a necessary means for church survival. And many people are finally becoming aware of this reality. The Pew Internet and American Life survey reveals that among churches that have a Web site, 83 percent say that it helps attract visitors to their church. Many of the churches reported that newcomers would visit only after looking at their church's Web site.[19] Numerous studies have also found that Internet users expect the Net to be a part of their religious experience. Simply put, not having a Web site is the equivalent of owning a business but not listing your phone number or address in any directories. Nevertheless—despite this overwhelming evidence—half the churches surveyed said they had no plans to develop a Web site in the future. *Amazing.* Here God has provided His people with such a versatile and effective tool, but many have chosen not to use it. God naturally blesses all mankind through his common grace (Matt. 5:45). Technology, properly used, is one of these blessings from God that can be used to glorify Him. Thus, it is high time we reversed the church's track record of ignoring technology and begin reaping the full potential of what Christ has given us—a tool to penetrate our society deeply and touch the lives of the saved and the lost, bringing them to the glory of Christ.

chapter seven

Understanding the Internet

The Internet is now a part of our everyday lives. We use it at work and at home, and with each passing day we become increasingly reliant on this technology. Whether performing our duties at work, shopping from home, or communicating with friends, we are spending more time online. And all indications are that this trend will continue for the foreseeable future.

With the increasing role that this medium is playing, it is now more important than ever that the church use it to bring unbelievers to Christ. But first we must have a solid understanding of the Internet. When we were young, we first had to learn to write our ABCs. Similarly, we must understand the fundamentals of the Internet to use the medium to its fullest.

In this chapter, we will focus on providing this foundation. More specifically, we will look at what the Internet is, its history, who is using it, and how it is being used. We will also tackle some of the misconceptions surrounding the Internet and why some people are afraid to use this God-given technology. This information will then lead us into the next chapter, in which we will explore eMinistry and learn how to use it to bring us—and those around us—closer to Christ.

What Is the Internet?

Webster's dictionary provides an excellent definition when it specifies the Internet as an "electronic communications network that connects computer networks and organizational computer facilities around the world." The *Columbia Encyclopedia* expands upon that definition, saying that the Internet is "an international computer network linking together thousands of individual networks at military and governmental agencies, educational institutions, nonprofit organizations, industrial and financial corporations of all sizes, and commercial enterprises that enable individuals to access the network." Putting it in laymen's terms, we can say that the Internet is a series of connected computers that share information. This information is sent from one source (the supplier) to another source (the recipient) and back if requested.[1]

Although many people have taken credit for the Internet, most authorities believe that J. C. R. Licklider conceived the Internet when he saw computers not only as machines for mathematical calculations and other similar uses but also as a powerful tool for communication. In 1968, he envisioned a machine whose "presence can change the nature and value of communication even more profoundly than did the printing press or picture tube."[2]

The actual building of the Internet began in 1969 with a secret U.S. government study, known as the Advanced Research Projects Agency network (ARPAnet). They initially intended for this study to be a test to find a system that could survive nuclear attacks. They began by connecting three networks from California to Utah, and by 1972 it had grown to include dozens of universities and research agencies as well.

But the real boom of the Internet did not occur until 1991, when Tim Berners-Lee introduced the World Wide Web. His doctoral work at the European Laboratory for Particle Physics (CERN) culminated in the development of a "browser" that linked documents to one another over the Internet. Use of this Web browser empowered individuals to "surf" through huge quantities of electronic data quickly and easily to find the information they sought. It was the "killer application" that the Internet needed, and the rest, as we say, is history.

Of course, any discussion of the Internet is incomplete without a review of another essential component of the Internet: e-mail. The term would appear to be a shorthand combination of the words *electronic* and *mail,* but some people contend that it derives from the French word *emmailleu're,* which means "network." Whichever explanation is true, e-mail can be defined as electronic mail sent from a sender to a recipient via the Internet. It is a quick, inexpensive, and convenient method of communication that allows us to stay in contact with each other more easily than by traditional communication methods.

We can trace the first instance of e-mail back to 1971 when Ray Tomlinson developed a way of sending himself a message through ARPAnet. From these humble beginnings, e-mail grew to become the most used application of the Internet. Today, it is becoming increasingly common for individuals to use e-mail instead of the phone to contact each other. And e-mail has become so integrated into our society that many people send dozens of e-mails a day. Billions of messages are sent each day, and the United States Postal Service estimates that more than four trillion messages are sent each year.

When discussing electronic communication, many people mistakenly refer to the World Wide Web as the Internet, and vice versa. But although the two systems are linked, they are not one and the same thing. The Web—and e-mail—are just two out of many parts of the Internet, but they do not comprise the entire Internet (fig. 1). Thus, throughout the rest of the book, we will refer to each component for what it is—the Internet as "the Internet" (or simply "the Net"), the World Wide Web as "the Web," and electronic mail (or *emmailleu're,* if you insist) as "e-mail."

COMPONENTS OF THE INTERNET

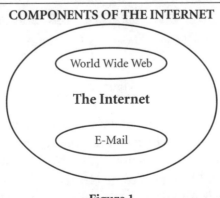

Figure 1

The combined forces of both the Web and e-mail create a powerful one-two punch. Next, we will examine who is using the Internet so that we may gain a better understanding of the people whom we can reach for Christ.

Who's Using the Internet?

The rapid growth of the Internet is a sure sign that we have a new vehicle for communication and content. The people who use it vary widely in age, race, and ethnicity, further indicating growth for an already-established medium. Therefore, one of our most critical areas of study is the demographics of the online world.

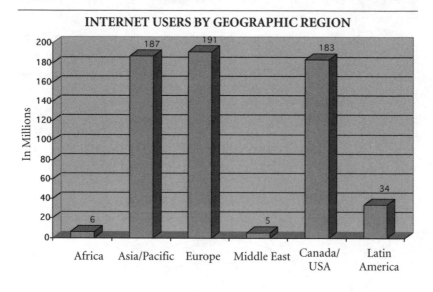

INTERNET USERS BY GEOGRAPHIC REGION

Figure 2

These citizens are lively inhabitants, actively involved on the Net and shaping it daily into a new place. Studies confirm that an over-whelming number of Internet users live in North America. According to The Media Audit, one-third of Net users—almost 200 million people—are either American or Canadian.[3] In the United States, 70

percent of white, 44 percent of African-American, 42 percent of His-
panic, and 70 percent of Asian households are connected, each quickly
embracing the Net (fig. 3).[4]

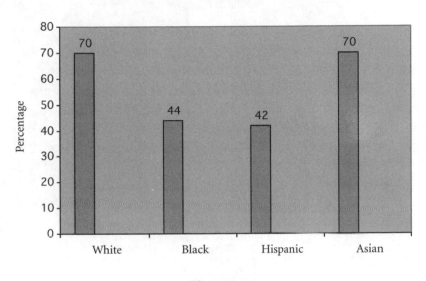

U.S. NET POPULATION BY ETHNICITY

Figure 3

Surprisingly, these groups are not as young as we might have assumed.
New evidence suggests that Net users over the age of twenty-five make
up a large part of the online population, though concentration is highest among those under thirty-five. We can surmise that the Net is not
yet dominated by our youth, but by the "digitally young"—people of all
ages who are technologically savvy. Collectively, 76 percent of those between the ages of 25 and 55 are "Net connected," both at home and at
work (fig. 4).

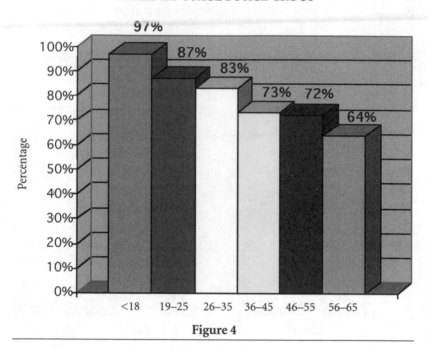

INTERNET USAGE BY AGE GROUP

Figure 4

Although many of the "Net-connected" are older, don't write off the younger generations just yet. Studies have found that the two fastest-growing segments of the Net populace are kids and teens. Of teens between the ages of 13 and 18, 97 percent are online![5] Nearly 100 percent of the high school graduating class of 2001 is connected, and nine out of ten use the Internet every day.[6]

The church must target this prime focus group as the group grows and prospers in the twenty-first century. As we saw in earlier chapters, America's youth are searching desperately for an identity that only Christ can provide. Fortunately, the Internet gives us a means for addressing their needs. The majority of teenage boys and girls say it is easier to discuss spiritual issues online than in the "real" world.[7] What a wonderful opportunity to reach these kids with tools such as the Web and e-mail.

Don Tapscott perhaps put it best when he wrote, "For the first time in history, children are more comfortable, knowledgeable, and literate than their parents about an innovation central to society. And it is through the use of the digital media that the Net Generation will develop and superimpose its culture on the rest of society. Boomers stand back. Already, these kids are learning, playing, communicating, working, and creating communities very differently than their parents. They are a force for social transformation."[8]

Although our focus here is mainly on Americans and their Internet usage, it is important not to ignore other parts of the world. Four hundred twenty-three million Internet users are outside of North America. These individuals need Christ every bit as much as we do, and they are an essential part of the future of the church. A great divide is growing between online ministries dedicated to reaching people outside the United States and ministries that are focusing within the United States. The most glaring need is for Web sites written in Spanish, German, Japanese, Chinese, and French. Our duty and obligation as God's church is to think of those people when we are developing an Internet evangelism strategy.

IN DEPTH Q AND A—PANTEGO BIBLE CHURCH

Site: www.pantego.org

Webmaster: Marty Hill

Pantego is a Bible church in Arlington, Texas, whose vision is to reach the 74 percent of unchurched people in their city. They will strive to fulfill this goal by establishing at least one fully functioning biblical community in the twenty high-school zones within a ten-mile radius of the church campus by the year 2010.

> Why was the Web site built? What are the goals of the site?

Although the vision of our Web site has taken on new characteristics and directions, the Pantego Bible Church Web site was originally envisioned as a communications vehicle from the church to the membership. While maintaining the original vision, it has also taken on the responsibility of representing our church throughout the world.

One of the original goals was to communicate events and information to the body by the fastest and easiest means possible while eliminating expensive printing and postage costs. Extending into our current goals, we also believe that the site must assist in, as well as show success in, the mission of our church, which is "Transforming people, through the work of the Holy Spirit, into fully developing followers of Christ." We assist people—members or not—in reaching this goal by offering online resources that will help in their daily walk. Some of these resources are offered free, such as our weekly study guides and streaming video of messages on various topics. These resources are now being used throughout the world, including such areas as New Zealand and Australia.

> Where did the inspiration for the Web site come from?

The current version of our site is inspired by the structure of our church. It is based upon a fourfold approach in helping one become a fully developing follower of Christ. We encourage each person to be involved in all four of the following areas: inspiration (worship services), instruction (community groups), involvement (home groups), and introspection (personal growth). All topics of study are based on what we call the Thirty Core Competencies, of which are ten beliefs, ten practices, and ten virtues that we believe must be a part of every Christian's life. These two areas, the fourfold approach, and the Thirty Core Competencies, are evident throughout the site.

> Who is your target audience? Is this matching your typical visitor?

Currently, our target audience is our congregation. However, we realize that many people access our site who do not go to Pantego. Therefore, we work to maintain the representation of the church. Most of our site is geared for the adult community, although we are working to make the youth and children's areas more attractive for them. Judging from the feedback we get on the site, we seem to be hitting the mark as far as the typical visitor is concerned.

> What kind of response are you receiving?

We are receiving very encouraging and positive responses, not only from church members but also others across the nation and the world.

> What are the most popular sections/features of the site?

The most popular area of our Web site by far is the free download of our study guide. Members download it, print it at home, and study it throughout the week for next Sunday's topic. The study guide itself is so good that other churches throughout the world are also using them. Currently, they are archived back to January 1, 2000.

Other areas of great interest are:

• the availability of streaming video for Sunday messages;

• the ordering of the Christian Life Profile, another resource that will help you determine where growth is needed in your life; and the Online Church Calendar.

> Have you seen any unexpected benefits of your Internet ministry?

Many of the things that have happened because of our Web

site are not unexpected. We've prayed for the Lord to enlarge our territory, and we strive to reach out to the world beyond our city boundaries. The Web site is just another tool to do that. However, we never cease to be awed when evidence of His work appears, such as positive responses about the site from others—both here at home and abroad—on how the use of our Web site enhanced their personal or their ministry's growth.

> Share one success story that has come from your Internet ministry.

Here is a quote from a message that we received from a seminary professor:

"I am really impressed with your Web site. It is extremely useful and does a great job of providing information. I have been using your church as an example church when teaching my classes, and you are definitely the best at using the Web in an incredibly creative way."

> What role do you think the Internet will play in the future of the church?

The Internet has become, for many people, the encyclopedia of the twenty-first century. If you need information, there is now no better place to go. If you have a topic, you can most likely find more than you could ever expect, assuming that you know where to look. Consequently, if I wish to find out more about a church, the first thing I do is look at their Web site. So, for attracting new members, a quality, informational Web site is a must. The site must include information that the typical Web surfer would be looking for if he or she came to your site for the first time.

For the members, the site must include not only timely information that will help them know what is going on in the church but also resources that will help them grow. Also, I predict that intrachurch communications will be commonplace in the near future. Some church sites have already moved into this phase of communication and, for example, members should be able to communicate with other members through the site for the purposes of emergency prayer chains and other needs.

> In the future, what would you like to see happen with the church on the Internet?

The church should be at the forefront of technology. In many areas, the church has been slow to adapt new ideas into its structure. A well-designed, innovative, state-of-the-art Web site can easily cost tens of thousands of dollars. However, many individuals (i.e., church members) possess knowledge in this area and can come alongside the church in a servanthood capacity by donating their time and energy to this idea. Although unavoidable costs are involved in producing and maintaining a quality Web site, programming costs can be kept to a minimum just by asking members of the body to help. Some people will go to school to learn how to do this.

That said, I would like to see churches being listed as top sites. By our being innovative and creative, our site should attract people to the church. It should say, "We are a church that uses everything we have for the Lord, and we use it to the very utmost of our capability. We strive to expand our gifts so that the Lord may be glorified and that lives may be changed."

> What suggestions do you have for those who want to build a ministry-based site?

I remember a time when I was a child. My family and I were in the car driving somewhere, and I noticed a construction site. This prompted me to ask my mother, "When are they going to be finished building the city?"

She replied, "They will never be finished building the city. As a city grows, there are always new things being built."

That same concept should be in place on a quality Web site. Keep it growing! Plan on the fact that there will *always* be a next phase. A site that gets completed is a dead site. People might come by once or even several times. But once they realize that nothing is new, they *will* move on. This is the "been-there-done-that" mentality. Plan in phases, and remember the KISS theory: "Keep it simple, Sam." Do not attempt to be the world's greatest site at the beginning. It's okay to plan long-term, but develop it methodically in measurable phases. Only thus will you feel the satisfaction that comes from knowing that the site is on its way toward being everything you wish it to be.

Getting into Web-page specifics, for ministries such as ours that have many departments, I recommend a dynamic structure with administrative pages configured for ministry leaders. This way, they maintain the content of their own ministry pages while you maintain control over the look and feel of the site. Such sites (of which ours is an example) are database driven. Pages are created dynamically from information entered by ministry leaders into the database via administrative pages. Our pages are written in Cold Fusion, which I also recommend. Between Cold Fusion, JavaScript, HTML, and SQL, there is not too much that you cannot do with a site. Throw in a little Flash animation, and you have a site that will rival any other site. Again, just the names of these languages can be intimidating, but, as I said earlier, that's why you should find church members who have gifts in these areas and use their expertise to build your site.

What Are Some Uses for the Internet?

Now that we have a better understanding of those who are using the Internet, we must understand why they use it and for what purposes. In these areas we can then look for points of leverage to advance the work of Christ.

People connect to the Internet to seek information and to communicate. These are the two principal realms in which the Internet thrives. No other single medium provides so much content, allows so much interactivity, and increases work productivity. With e-mail and the World Wide Web, there is no limit to what can be done. And we are only beginning to realize all of the possible applications.

In a recent study, researchers at UCLA found that the most common Net activities were e-mail and instant messaging, Web browsing, finding entertainment, purchasing products online, and reading the news.[9] All of these uses represent the keys to the Internet's success and are prime examples of how individuals spend their time online. Communication and information are the pillars upon which much of the future technology will be built.

The Internet Is Used for Communication

Just a decade ago, letters and phone calls were our primary means of long-distance communication. But now the phenomena of e-mail and instant messaging are replacing more traditional means of communication. Trillions of e-mail messages are sent each year, and nearly half of all Americans send at least one e-mail each day. Teenagers are using instant messaging at an ever-increasing rate. As a recent report found, "Talking to buddies has become the information-age way for teens to hang out and beat back boredom."[10]

The Net has enabled us to communicate more easily, keep in contact with those we normally couldn't, and meet people we otherwise wouldn't. As with all good technology, these advantages are not passing Internet users by. A recent study found that of all of the activities in which Net users partake online, communicating with others is what they enjoy the most.[11] They are ecstatic about this newfound ability, and multitudes are setting aside pen and paper to use e-mail as their primary means of communication. With a single e-mail address and the click of a mouse, we can reach anyone in the world from the comfort of our home or workplace. This ease of use is second to none, and companies such as Nokia and Motorola are now enabling us to use more traditional items such as cell phones and pagers to send text messages. As a result, individuals can now communicate more easily with their loved ones and share their lives more closely with those they choose. Perhaps the best part of all is the incremental cost associated with e-mail: virtually nothing.

Citizens of the Web—also known as "Netizens"—are also finding new friends online, some of whom they might never meet in person. Through technologies such as chat rooms and bulletin boards, Internet users can have discussions with new people and enjoy casual conversations about their favorite subjects. It is possible to find a person to chat with about nearly anything, as new Web sites pop up every day that focus on the most esoteric of subjects. Users enjoy the anonymity that the Internet provides, and many people draw on this medium as an opportunity to express their true selves without the social pressures they would normally face.

Countless people find friends they haven't seen for years or whom they could not contact via traditional means. With online directories and ubiquitous "people searches," it is increasingly commonplace to hear of high-school sweethearts or a group of best friends meeting again for the first time in years. Services are available that offer a way to find old schoolmates, those who have moved to foreign lands, and even old army pals. One such service allows users to search for POWs and people who are considered missing in action. No matter what the need, a way now exists to find just about any individual who was once close to us.

The opportunities afforded by e-mail and the Internet are endless, and as connectivity increases, so will communication. The explosion of e-mail and instant messaging is changing the world as we know it, and we are truly living in a communication-based world. But we are also living in a world that is increasingly information-driven. Let's investigate this aspect of the Net and find out why information is becoming the pot of gold at the end of the online rainbow.

The Internet Is Used for Information

Information is what makes the World Wide Web go around. More people use the Web to seek out information than for any other purpose. Information is the hot new Internet commodity, and consumers hunt for information as if it were their lifeblood. It is the primary reason that people connect themselves and their families to the Net. Companies everywhere are fighting each other to find the best ways to provide this emerging market with the services it needs.

We are a society that is becoming increasingly reliant upon information for survival, and the initial results of this trend are positive. Students rely on the Internet instead of the library for preparing school reports. The result? Grades begin to rise. Teachers find ideas for new projects and methods of communication. The result? The classroom receives a much-needed boost of creativity. Workers seek new and streamlined ways to provide customers with their product. The result? Companies achieve higher earnings, and their employees become more knowledgeable.

Much of this might not come as a surprise. Many people have heard the nightly news reports, read the newspaper articles, and watched the commercials heralding the Internet as the "information superhighway." One can seemingly find anything on the Web today, much of it trivial. But what exactly is the information that people seek most? Entertainment? Products? Career advice? News? These topics certainly are popular, but they are not the most prevalent, according to the Pew Internet and American Life Project. Their most recent study found that 25 percent of Internet users and twenty-eight million Americans have used the Internet to find religious information and materials and that up to three million people search for this material every day.[12] The study reports, "It is interesting to note that more people have gotten religious or spiritual information online than have gambled online, used

Web auction sites, traded stocks online, placed phone calls on the Internet, done online banking, or used Internet-based dating services."[13] This is good news for the church and a further indication that we live in a society that is starved for spirituality.

The events of September 11, 2001, also confirm this fact. On that day and shortly thereafter, nearly half of all Internet users sent or received e-mail prayer requests. Through e-mail, inspirational chain letters and personal requests for prayer spread quickly across the world, and countless individuals logged on to find information about Islam. But most people used the Internet to contact others with whom they could relate. Bulletin boards, chat rooms, and newsgroups were immediately set up, not only for those who experienced loss that day but also for those who felt the emotional turmoil of such a tragic event. America was a country in search of both itself and strength, and we found it in God. It is amazing to watch Christ use the Internet as such a crucial resource during these times. It is proof that He uses the technology around us for the good of His people.

With the Net's information and communication capabilities, we stand on the threshold of a new world. The Internet is full of "religion surfers," and their number continues to rise. Consequently, the church's road to relevancy goes through them. But this road is full of potholes—concerns and fears that threaten to keep the church from using the Internet for Christ. These are largely misconceptions, issues that the church must face to reach both believers and nonbelievers for Christ. Let us now examine—and begin to put to rest—some of the major misconceptions surrounding the Internet.

What Are Some Common Misconceptions About the Internet?

To this point, we have focused largely on the good that the Internet has brought to our world. But some Christians are fearful of the Internet, choosing to overlook the positives to focus solely on the negatives. These individuals insist that the Internet is a secular medium that has no place in the church. They point out pornographic Web sites and stories they have heard about criminals using the Internet for the detriment of society. Because of fear, they throw the baby out with the bathwater and disparage a medium that God has provided to reach new generations for Christ. This fear, if not addressed, can spread quickly through our congregations and choke any chance we have of using the Internet for the work that Christ has placed before us. But what is the root of this fear? Much of it is rooted in misinformation that is fed by the media, friends and family members. Horror stories and bad experiences make the best stories and always gain a lot of publicity and exposure. This is true with the Internet as well.

But the main answer lies primarily in the ambiguous nature of the Net. From books to magazines, from medical information to the location of a doctor's office, all kinds of information is readily available. This wide spectrum of available information exemplifies the diverse nature of the Net (and the Web particularly) and is one reason the Net is so valuable. But this variety also creates problems, one of which is that it's difficult to know what you're going to get when you click on a link. It's also often difficult to ascertain the accuracy and validity of much of what is posted on the Net. Because it is such an inexpensive medium, almost anyone can put up whatever they please on their Web sites. Some sites use this freedom to promote and show pornographic, blasphemous, or other harmful materials, degrading the very nature of the Web and bringing down the trust that we have in the medium. But even "clean" sites can be filled with erroneous and unsubstantiated information.

Another problem on the Web is that widely differing sites can have very similar addresses. The Web employs a system that recognizes Web addresses by the last few letters in their name, such as .com (for commercial enterprises), .net (for network systems), .gov (for government sites), and .org (for nonprofit organizations). But not everyone conforms to these address guidelines. Although many organizations buy the Web address they want, another company, organization, or individual may buy one of the other available alternatives and use it for their own purposes. A good example is the White House Web site. The government registered www.whitehouse.gov as its official address, but they didn't register the same address ending in .com, .net, or .org. Imagine the surprise in store for a Web user who types in www.whitehouse.com and finds himself at a XXX pornography site. Only www.whitehouse.gov will take a user to the White House's official site.

Undoubtedly, a darker side of the Net exists, one that can be used for evil, greed, and the harm of others. Pornography abounds on the Web and, as in life, there are people waiting to take advantage of those who use the Web. Complicating matters further, many magazines have spread heavy doses of misinformation by running lead stories on the addictive nature of the Web and the pornographic material that it contains (only 3.3 percent of Web sites contain such material).[14] With wildly exaggerated headlines, these articles have spread fear among many people and kept them from seeing the real use of the Internet. With such cases abounding on the Web today, no wonder some individuals shy away from using the Net altogether. So how do we address these issues, and what should we do?

As a Christian community, we can not simply ignore the Internet. This inaction would be a major folly; only through education and an understanding of the medium can we begin to ease the fear of the Internet that some people in the Christian community face. The Net has a large influence on our society, yet rarely do we hear it mentioned during church services or programs. It is time to start addressing the Internet during these times and educate our congregations to both the good and the bad of the Internet. Pastors might encourage small classes devoted to getting church members accustomed to the Net. No better place exists for an individual to learn than at church, under the supervision and instruction of a fellow Christian.

But perhaps the best way to show how the Internet can be used for good is by example. Nearly 50 percent of "religion surfers" report an improvement in their spiritual life, and even more report that church Web activities improve congregational life.[15] By implementing a successful Internet strategy for your church, we can begin changing the hearts and minds of doubters, simultaneously fulfilling our obligations under Christ. After all, in reaching people for Christ, we haven't ignored print and video media, both of which can also be used for evil.

With our newfound understanding, we have laid the foundation for using the Internet to fulfill the Great Commission. This, in turn, will help the church become culturally relevant in our society. The key to reaching new generations for Christ lies in the building of eMinistry.

chapter eight

Putting the Internet to Work for Christ

So far we have studied the importance of the Internet to our society and how it has changed us in ways previously unseen. We have also gained a solid understanding of the Internet, its history, who is using it, and how it is being used. But where is all of this leading? Where do we go from here? Most importantly, how might we put this information to work for Christ and His church?

This chapter will focus on these subjects as we explore eMinistry and ways to use it to further the cause of Christ. Along the way, we will look at the various kinds of eMinistry with their benefits and advantages; suggestions will be given on how to start a church Web site on a limited budget and with little expertise. Let's begin by looking at eMinistry, its applications, and the benefits in using it for Christ's work.

What Is eMinistry?

The word *eMinistry* has many different meanings. But for our purposes we can simply define it as using the Internet and related technology to minister both to lost and saved people. Although it is not intended to replace other existing forms of ministry, eMinistry focuses on the use of the most powerful and influential technology of our current age. Be assured that eMinistry will change the way we communicate and evangelize in the not-so-distant future. And eMinistry applications will provide low-cost and improved communications among congregations and church communities. This open dialogue made possible by Internet technology will strengthen the church family and bring us closer to people of distant locations and cultures.

How Can eMinistry Help Your Church?

Indeed, eMinistry provides for more effective missions and evangelism ministries, allowing us to reach those who otherwise would be unreachable. Individuals and families who are new to Christianity or have recently moved to a new location are often shy about visiting a new church. Many of us remember the difficulty that we experienced in beginning at a new school or meeting coworkers at a new job. We can make the same case for visiting a new church. Susan Gibbs, a spokeswoman for the Catholic Archdiocese has found that "a lot of people are very uncomfortable opening the door to a church and walking in alone. The Web lets them open that door."[1]

Another way that eMinistry can help is to alleviate cultural and geographical gaps that are such a hindrance to evangelism efforts. Because Web sites and e-mail are truly worldwide, a small church in Omaha, Nebraska, can lead Estonians to salvation through their eMinistry efforts. A large church in Dallas, Texas, can lead Islamic groups in the Middle East to Christ through their online plan of salvation. A newly planted church in San Jose, California, can reach Japanese kids through their message boards, and a youth group in New York can minister to adults in Chicago.

These examples are all possible because eMinistry allows for a sense of community, privacy, and open dialogue. The sharing of spiritual stories and reflection among Christians can be of great influence to unbelievers seeking redemption, especially among our youth. The privacy of reading Christian material at home on our own computers sets a comfortable environment for unbelievers to review Christianity anonymously and without pressure. Holding open discussions with believers on message boards eliminates many social fears that unbelievers have. Those of other faith groups can even read the Bible online and easily contact a church with questions that they might have. Table 1 offers ideas about how congregations can use the Web in ministry.

WHAT CONGREGATIONS DO WITH THEIR WEB SITES

Feature	Currently offers this feature
Encourage visitors to attend their church	83%
Post mission statements, sermons, or other text concerning faith	77%
Links to denomination and faith-related sites	76%
Links to Scripture studies or devotional material	60%
Post schedules, meeting times, and internal communications for the church	56%
Post photos of congregational events	50%
Post youth group material	44%
Has material promoting missionary evangelical work	31%
Seeks volunteers for congregational work	19%
Provides space for prayer requests	18%
Has a sign-up feature for classes/programs	8%
Allows online fundraising	5%
Webcasts worship services	4%
Provides discussion space for study or prayer groups	3%

Source: Pew Internet & American Life Project Religion Surfers Survey, July 24–August 15, 2001.

Table 1

Will eMinistry revolutionize the way the church will function? Barna Research answers this question with a resounding, "Yes!" Their studies indicate that more than two-thirds of people surveyed were likely to engage regularly in religious experiences online as the decade progresses.[2]

Ken Bedell of the United Methodist Church found that nearly 80 percent of people surveyed confirmed that the Internet already plays a significant role in their spiritual life.[3] This data confirms many other studies that have found similar results, and, so far, all indications are that they are correct. But these positive findings do not come without bad news. Looking at the Web, one easily finds that churches lack an eMinistry presence; and it is hard to find any churches that are implementing strategies successfully. This fact shows a serious lack of church presence on the Internet today. So, how can we fix this situation and provide our church with a high-impact presence on the Net?

How Can the Church Have a High-Impact Internet Presence?

The answer lies in the aggressive creation of church Web sites and applying new and existing methods of eMinistry. Most of these methods fall into two categories—communicative and informational.

Communicative eMinistry

The first category of eMinistry is based on communication. Whether it is church members passing along prayer requests or missionaries sending requests for donations, all forms of eMinistry in this category share a common trait—communication between saved and unsaved individuals. The following sections will identify particular eMinistries, provide Web sites that illustrate the ministry well, and continue on to explain how the ministry functions.

1. Prayer-Based eMinistry

Examples: www.eprayer.org, www.crosswalk.com
Prayer ministry is one of the most common Net-based activities. It

usually takes the form of a Web site that focuses on the existing con-gregation of a church or e-mail that is passed among a preset list of people. Predominate uses of prayer-based eMinistry include personal prayer requests, church prayer requests, and prayer updates posted on a Web site or sent via e-mail.

Prayer-based eMinistry offers many benefits, not the least of which is convenience. Nearly half of all religious Web users have found prayer resources more available on the Web than offline. Consistent prayer updates are available throughout the week, and church members can go to a Web site to view status updates whenever and wherever they wish. Many churches even recruit individuals to handle prayer requests and post them on a Web page when appropriate. For example, in the introduction to this book, we mentioned the ministry of Mary, the "prayer lady" who was confined to a wheelchair in a nursing home.

2. Community-Based eMinistry

Examples: www.theooze.com, www.christianity.com

Community-based eMinistry typically takes the form of Web sites for churches and their local community or small groups. Reports in-dicate that church schedules, calendars, and bulletins are the most read sections of a church's Web site. Many of them use event sign-up lists, discussion groups, e-mail lists, and chat rooms to facilitate conversa-tion, pass important church information (such as class times and dates), and heighten a sense of community within the church and lo-cal areas. Many churches even network their Web site with the sites of other like-minded churches and organizations, creating a broad, Web-based community.

This sharing of ideas, thoughts, and stories among those who know each other both on- and offline is a great spiritual motivator. Chat rooms and message boards help facilitate this sharing. The Pew Internet and American Life Project found that "by creating better ties within a preexisting community, by creating a Web presence, and by facilitating discussions that can be difficult to hold in other settings, congregations tightened bonds with their groups, reestablished connections with former members, and in some cases, expanded their missions on a global scale."[4]

People also use e-mail quite often in community-based eMinistry. Pew reports that 91 percent of the people say that e-mail has helped church members stay more in touch with one another, and 63 percent say that it has helped the congregation connect with the surrounding community more effectively.[5] Many churches provide sign-up sheets at church meetings, classes, and functions that allow members to receive e-mail each week with church information (e.g., class times, sermon notes, and church news and events) and weekly devotionals and pastoral encouragement.

3. Evangelism-Based eMinistry

Examples: www.servantevangelism.com, www.evangelismtoolbox.com

Evangelism-based eMinistry is primarily for seekers and the unsaved. Andrew, the twenty-five-year-old who was mentioned in the introduction to this book, was witnessing online to Mark, a seeker who had rarely been to church. Evangelism-based eMinistry provides easy access to evangelistic Bible teaching, plans of salvation, Q and A's, and contact information. Many seekers will first visit a church's Web site rather than the church itself, because they have a high fear factor that the Web, fortunately, can help alleviate. Nearly half of all religious surfers visit Web sites to find information about religions other than their own.

According to field research done by Arne Fjeldstad, 44.5 percent of churches surveyed have seen their Internet ministry lead one or more people to Christ.[6] Many churches do this through tracts that have Web addresses printed on them. Others use Web sites that lead the seeker through the plan of salvation. What a powerful weapon in the church's arsenal!

Teens are getting in on this form of evangelism as well. Andrew Careaga has found that "Christian teens who are active in the discussions [of online discussion groups] often see the Internet as a tool to help fulfill the mandate to evangelize and make disciples of non-

Christians."[7] Many of us who have worked with teens know that getting them involved in church is difficult. With the Internet, however, they are not only doing Christ's work but also doing it in an environment they like and are comfortable with.

When both teens and church groups use eMinistry, a great transformation of the church's evangelistic strategy takes place, one that uses church resources more readily and reaches more people while simultaneously bringing the church into the Information Age. Unifying our knowledge of Scripture and the strength of Christ's workers with Internet ministry is a powerful way to touch those who seemed unreachable and lead them to Him.

4. Missions-Based eMinistry

Examples: www.namb.net, www.caminternational.org

Missions-based eMinistry helps missionaries or missionary organizations connect with their supporters and others who are interested in their ministry. Their Web sites often contain profiles, contact information, prayer requests, donation lists, and more. Several missions organizations have even used their Web sites successfully to raise money. Often, though, the benefit of this form of eMinistry lies in the support they receive from the church.

Perhaps the most useful aspect of missions-based eMinistry is how it links missionaries to churches and the outside world. Whereas in the past they might have been isolated, e-mail now provides them with an easy and inexpensive method of communication. In remote areas, where long-distance calling is prohibitively expensive, e-mail can be of great service, keeping the missionaries in contact with their sponsoring church and individual supporters. Also, with missions-based eMinistry, church members can e-mail the missionaries and see status updates, what they need, and how they can be prayed for, all daily. Susan, the woman mentioned in the introduction, was involved in a missions-based eMinistry in her seventy-five-member church. This situation is quite a turnaround from just fifty years ago, when churches often didn't hear from missionaries for months or even years at a time.

RELIGIOUS SURFERS' FAVORITE SITE FEATURES

Feature	Uses feature	Does not use feature	Feature not available to user	Doesn't know or refused to answer
Information about their own faith or religion	67%	13%	18%	2%
Information about social issues	44%	20%	26%	10%
Guided meditations, devotionals, or other material for personal prayer	41%	20%	29%	10%
Books, music, or other religious material for sale	35%	38%	21%	7%
Information about different faiths or religions	16%	13%	66%	5%
Interactive prayer requests and responses	15%	24%	48%	13%
Chat rooms and bulletin boards	12%	27%	43%	18%
Regular online worship services	5%	8%	74%	13%

Source: Pew Internet & American Life Project Religion Surfers Survey, July 24–August 15, 2001.

Table 2

Informational eMinistry

The second category of eMinistry is based on information. Informational eMinistry focuses on teaching, church-related activities and events, and Christian resources, many of which are difficult to find offline. With a common thread of information distribution, each form of information eMinistry provides Christians and non-Christians alike with biblical resources anytime, anywhere. As with our discussion of communicative eMinistry, the following sections will identify particular eMinistries, provide one or two examples of Web sites that illustrate the ministry well, and then explain how the ministry serves people.

1. Teaching-Based eMinistry

Examples: www.pantego.org, http://www.bible.org

Barna research indicates that Internet users prefer online teaching to any other online religious endeavor.[8] Teaching-based eMinistry includes downloadable audio or video sermons, daily devotionals, and weekly church bulletins that people may access online via a Web site or e-mail. The advantage of this form of eMinistry is its constant availability to those who want to access it on their own time. It is also of great benefit for people who are unable to attend church on Sundays—whether for health, job, or family reasons.

Teaching-based eMinistry is especially attractive to young Internet users. Studies show that people under the age of thirty-five are its most accepting users. Barna predicts that by the end of the decade, up to one hundred million individuals, mostly youth, will be listening to sermons online from their local church or other, more distant, churches.[9] After all, distance makes no difference on the Internet, thereby creating prime opportunities for small churches to reach people worldwide.

2. Church-Based eMinistry

Examples: www.willowcreek.org, www.lakepointe.org

Church-based eMinistry revolves around a church and its beliefs, schedules, activities, and events. Many churches say that their people read these listings more often than any other portion of their Web site, and it's easy to see why. Congregants can quickly and easily view the schedules, youth group material, and event listings of their churches, including vacation Bible school, picnics, mission trips, community socials, and church restoration projects. These sites allow congregants to stay attuned to and abreast of their church's activities.

Many churches place a summary of spiritual beliefs on their Web site so that visitors can view where the church stands on biblical issues. Increasingly, we see newcomers attending a church only after first visiting its Web site and reading this information. This fact demonstrates the important role that the Internet is playing in matters of the church, and exemplifies the necessity of good, accurate Web-site content.

3. Resource-Based eMinistry

Examples: www.gospelcom.net, www.pastors.com

Although it is not church-specific, another form of eMinistry is resource based. Similar to an online store, various sites sell and distribute religious items through eCommerce. These items include Bibles, study guides, trinkets, and nearly anything else under the sun. Many of these sites specialize in selling unique or hard-to-find resources, such as out-of-print books or custom-made religious T-shirts.

Other resource-based eMinistries choose the noncommercial route, providing free access to their content. Downloadable sermon illustrations, Web-site tools, and links to other faith-based Web sites, as well as information about social issues are just a few of the common applications used in this form of eMinistry. However, some Web sites are simply depositories for various religious texts, similar to a library. Whether free or at cost, resource-based eMinistries allow Internet users easy access to materials that they otherwise would have difficulty obtaining.

ACTIVITIES OF ONLINE RELIGIOUS SURFERS

Looked for information about their own faith	67%
Looked for information about another faith	50%
E-mailed a prayer request	38%
Given spiritual guidance via e-mail	37%
Bought religious items online	34%
Planned religious activities via e-mail	29%
Downloaded sermons	25%
Sought spiritual guidance via e-mail	21%
Gone online to find a new church	14%
Participated in online worship	4%

Source: Pew Internet & American Life Project Religion Surfers Survey, July 24–August 15, 2001.

Table 3

Applying these methods of eMinistry and creating Web sites aggressively will begin to improve the church's presence on the Web. The more we can establish effective Web sites, the more we can reach people for Christ. Chances are good that people will visit your Web site before they will visit your church, so it had better be good. Most individuals, though, do not have the technical expertise or know-how to create a Web site and begin their eMinistry. It is not uncommon to hear someone ask, "How do I build a Web site and get e-mail with little money and without much expertise?"

Instruction on building a Web site is outside the scope of this book; fortunately, many services and resources are available to help, whether you are building the Web site yourself or hiring someone else to do it. Appendix

B lists several companies that will build a Web site for you or provide easy-to-use Web page templates that you can publish yourself. It also contains a list of books that will assist you in building a Web site on your own. These are tried-and-true resources that will help you with the difficult task that lies ahead. Finally, it lists several Internet service providers (ISPs) that will host your Web site and give you e-mail so that your eMinistry is complete. I have provided the costs of these services along with each listing.

IN-DEPTH Q AND A—CAM INTERNATIONAL

Site: www.caminternational.org

Webmaster: Aaron Sandoval

CAM International is a missions organization focused on reaching individuals in Spanish-speaking parts of the world.

> Why was the Web site built?

As a recruitment tool. We wanted to be able to reach those who are seeking involvement in missions and provide them with an informative and intuitive source on how they also can get involved.

> Where did the inspiration for the site originate?

Many secular sites are taking advantage of the Internet's potential to create a user experience as they push their product or agenda. We thought that a need existed to take advantage of this as well by allowing prospective missionaries to get a feel for what the mission field is like.

> What are the goals of the site?

We have several. We want to:

• increase our communication with prospective recruits;

• help these recruits by providing a pool of opportunities in which they can get involved (while educating them about these opportunities);

• help potential recruits as they begin the process of determining God's will for their lives, assisting in any way that we can; and

• communicate a new image for CAM International—an image of a ministry leader.

> Who is your target audience? Does this match your typical visitor?

Our target is college/seminary students or recent graduates who are looking for opportunities to get involved in missions. Unfortunately, many of the campuses we hope to target have not responded accordingly. We are, however, trying to increase our traffic through offline awareness programs that feature the Web site.

> What kind of response are you receiving?

We are currently communicating with about 650 different people daily, making the Web our most useful recruiting tool. Our goal is to eventually reach 2,000 visitors each day.

> What are the most popular sections/features of the site?

It would have to be our searchable database of ministry opportunities. Visitors appreciate the ability to see a current list of places or ministries where they can serve. This feature allows them to get a good idea of what to expect and how they can serve. For example, through a customizable feature called "MyOpps," visitors are able to store and review their favorite ministry opportunities and apply for any services directly related to that opportunity.

> How do you think the church is faring on the Internet today?

Generally speaking, I don't believe that the church has quite grasped the concept of the Internet yet. Many people still see it as a toy, a generational thing, or as a diversion. They fail to see it strategically or to understand the incredible potential that it offers. It's not just about a Web site, many of which are just online brochures. It's not just about cyberspace. It is about taking the strategy and the potential behind the technology to further our purpose and our mission.

> What role do you think the Internet will play in the future of the church?

I think the Internet must play a huge role in the future of the church. If it is used properly, this technology will allow us to have better tools in the pursuit of our mission. It will probably change our perception and use of older media, transforming the way the church communicates and operates. However, it does not change our message but allows us to share it faster, louder, farther, and better.

> What would you like to see happen with the church on the Internet?

I would like to see the church understand the true nature of the medium and use it wisely. I would like to see the church close distances and exploit technologies that allow us to reach beyond our traditional grasp.

> What suggestions do you have for those who want to build a ministry-based site?

They must understand that the Internet is only a tool to help further their mission. They must first establish their mission and purpose, and then use the available tools. Technology should not drive ministry, but ministry should determine the technology that we use. Seek to be professional in all you do, including use of the Internet.

How Do You Begin an eMinistry?

No doubt you are beginning to envision the different types of eMinistry that your church might pursue. New roads of ministry are beginning to open before your very eyes. You can practically see the new facility that you will need just to hold all of your church's new congregants.

But not so fast! You'll need to take certain steps that will decide the success of your new eMinistry. These steps are crucial to providing focus and direction, and only by taking them will you begin to build the successful eMinistry that you envision.

What are these steps? We will concentrate on several preliminary steps to take in beginning your eMinistry. With this information as a foundation, you can then explore the many excellent resources at your local bookstore and on the Web for further instruction. (See appendix B for suggestions.)

Choose an Effective Domain Name

A *domain name* is another term for a Web-site address. When you open your Internet browser and type in the name of a Web site that you would like to visit—for example, www.ESPN.com—you are typing in a domain name. Choosing a good name is a key consideration when planning your Web site, and you should always attempt to find one that is accurate, descriptive, and succinct. Never make it difficult for a visitor to find your site. If the name of your church is Washunk Baptist Fellowship, choosing www.washunkbaptist.com is a good choice for your Web site's domain name and address (URL). Keeping the domain name short will allow visitors to find and access your site easily and limit the possibility of spelling errors. Often, however, a Web-site name will already be registered to another church, business, or person. You will then have to look for alternatives. How do you know when this is the case? By visiting VeriSign's Web site.

VeriSign (www.verisign.com) is a company that provides domain name look-up and registration services. When you visit their site, you can search for any name and determine if it is available. If it is available, you can register it and the name will be yours for a predetermined amount of time. If someone has already purchased the name you want, you must begin to think of alternate names to register. In these cases, the best idea is to find a variant name that will suit your ministry. In the preceding example, Washunk Baptist Fellowship could register www.washunkchurch.com if their first choice is not available.

It is always best to register a .com domain name. Although many other variations are available (e.g., .net and .org), .com is the most widely used and the domain name extension that most visitors will try first. A technique that many professionals suggest is to register as many names that are similar to yours as possible. In our example, Washunk Baptist could register www.washunkchurch.com, www.washunkchurch.net, and www.washunkchurch.org. This way, visitors are not confused about how to find your site.

Choose an Effective Team

Unless you are building the Web site yourself, have an experienced Web development team put together a site for you. They are not only seasoned pros but also will help you make the best decisions during the site building process. Scott Thumma reports in a Hartford Institute study, "Many of the [church] sites surveyed could have benefited from professional design assistance."[10] Churches commonly try to save time and money by choosing the cheapest or easiest Web-design companies available. However, in the long run it usually results in twice the expense and an inferior product. Much can be said about getting a great Web site produced the first time around.

Hiring the right team of professionals can be a tricky task. Skill, experience, creative talent, and technical expertise must be abundant.

Finding all of these qualities in one team or person is the goal. Search the Web for development companies in your area, and schedule a time to sit down with them. Be up front about your budget and have a list ready of what you would like to see on your site. Review this material with them carefully, and ask to see examples of their work and references from past clients. Remember that hiring a team is difficult, and good references can go a long way toward putting your mind at ease.

It is wise to put together a Web development team within your church. The creation of a new kind of church staff or Web team will help keep the site fresh, updated, and free from bugs. These individuals can then dedicate themselves to building the best eMinistry possible for your church. Also consider developing a staff position, such as pastor of eMinistry or director of Internet ministries. Ken Bedell describes this new pastor as "primarily a listener and not a proclaimer. . . . Skills of hearing spiritual issues and connecting them to faith stories are more important than being able to present doctrine clearly. Telling stories is more important than preaching. Empathy is more important than analysis. Dialogue is more important than dogma."[11] The traditional role that a pastor has played in the church of the past does not fit the eMinistry of the present. A new kind of leader must handle eMinistry, bringing a more effective evangelism to upcoming generations.

Set a Formal Strategy

Churches should always think of their eMinistry as an ongoing process, not a simple, one-time commitment. Consequently, it is important to develop a formal strategy for your eMinistry before it begins. Internet users will notice and appreciate a well thought out and well-planned Web site. The worst strategy in building a Web site is simply to throw one up. It will do much damage and harm your church's credibility.

A good Web-development company should be able to help you with this task, but it is still a good idea to be familiar with the strategy-creation process so that you are prepared for what lies ahead. This

familiarity is even more important for those people who are planning
to create an eMinistry themselves.

The Yale Web Style Guide succinctly outlines the following steps to
take before creating a Web site:

- Know your purpose.
- Know your objectives.
- Know your target audience.
- Know your content.

The purpose of your eMinistry and each of its components should
always be clear and well-defined. Far too many people who create Web
sites are not exactly sure why they are doing so. Writing down a purpose statement protects you and gives your eMinistry purpose from
the start. It also guarantees that everyone on your development team
is on the same page, working toward a common goal.

Give top priority to knowing your eMinistry objectives. By creating goals, you can set standards and measure your success. Otherwise,
you might find yourself with a purposeless Web site, something that
no one wants and no one is interested in. For example, if a church's
eMinistry is evangelism based, they should set a goal for the number
of people to reach each month and year. If a church's eMinistry is community based, the goal should be to increase attendance at church functions by church members and people from the local community. Also,
make these goals realistic to avoid discouraging those who are involved
in creating the eMinistry.

Of course, a key to knowing your eMinistry's purpose and objectives is to know your target audience. Who are the people you're trying to reach? Where do they live, and what are their interests? These
are essential questions to answer. To obtain this information, you must
first know the type of eMinistry your church will develop (thus the
importance of learning the different eMinistry types discussed above).

With your objectives and purpose in hand and your audience clearly
defined, it is vital to know the content of the Web site that you will
build. Whether you are working with a team or on your own, outlin-

ing the information on the site will help at each step along the way. Simply create an outline and fill it in with each component of the site, page by page. Start big with every conceivable idea and only later pare this down to what is actually possible. By doing so, you will firmly establish direction and enhance understanding of the Web site.

Additional Suggestions

It is impossible to overemphasize the importance of dedicating appropriate time and resources to your eMinistry. Consider devoting a fixed and consistent time to it each week. You can spend this time answering e-mail, updating a Web site, implementing changes and suggestions, and improving the eMinistry's overall effectiveness. Also, begin collecting resources for your eMinistry. Ensure that eMinistry is a line item in the budget. You might consider holding church fundraisers to gain the resources needed for your eMinistry to flourish and grow over time.

While building your eMinistry Web site, ensure effective communication by writing clearly and concisely. Check your grammar and spelling, and, if possible, use professional writers. It is well worth the cost of hiring a freelance writer so your visitor doesn't have to encounter embarrassing copy errors.

Also, do not assume that visitors know about Christ, the Bible, and His sacrifice for us. Although many people might already know these things, some of them will not. Allow the purpose and meaning of your eMinistry to shine through to limit confusion on the part of visitors. A clear declaration of your mission and purpose will reflect positively upon the site and your church.

Finally, practice what you preach. If you say it on the Web site, you must do it at church. Visitors will develop certain expectations after visiting the site, and your ministry should meet these when the people actually attend the church. Otherwise, they are likely to leave frustrated or angry and not return.

The Great Commission is still viable in the twenty-first century; thus we would be wise to use twenty-first century methods to reach the saved and the lost. God's challenge for us lies ahead and we can charge forward by using the Internet as a ministry tool. Let us not ignore this tool, but use it to bring us closer to the glory of Christ

Sites That Do It Right

The following is a list of Web sites that are superb examples of eMinistry in action. Please note that at time of publication, all links are active and working. Due to the evolving nature of Web sites, some links may move or change.

Churches and Ministries

Crosswalk.com
www.crosswalk.com

ePrayer
www.eprayer.com

Ginghamsburg Church
http://www.ginghamsburg.org

Grace Community Church
http://www.gccaz.org/

The Highway Community
http://www.highway.org

Journey
http://www.journeydallas.com

The Journey
http://www.nyjourney.com/

Lake Pointe Baptist Church
http://www.lakepointe.org/

Mars Hill Fellowship
http://www.marshillchurch.org

Mosaic
http://www.mosaic.org

The Next Level
http://www.tnl.org/

Next-Wave
http://www.next-wave.org/

Pantego Bible Church
http://www.pantego.org

Saddleback Community Church
http://www.saddleback.com

University Baptist Church
http://www.ubc.org

Warehouse
http://www.warehouse242.org

Willow Creek Community Church
http://www.willowcreek.org

Wooddale Community Church
http://www.wooddale.org

Xenos
http://www.xenos.org/

Mission Organizations

CAM International
http://www.caminternational.org

Global Mission Fellowship
http://www.gmf.org/

Gospel for Asia
http://www.gfa.org/

Miami Rescue Mission
http://www.caringplace.org

New Tribes Mission
http://www.ntm.org/

North American Mission Board
http://www.namb.net/

Church and Ministry Resources

Biblical Studies Foundation
http://www.bible.org/

Christians Online
http://www.christianity.com

Evangelism Toolbox
http://www.evangelismtoolbox.com/

GospelCom
http://www.gospelcom.net

The Leadership Network
http://www.leadnet.org/

The Malphurs Group
http://www.malphursgroup.com

TheOoze
http://www.theooze.com

Pastors.com
http://www.pastors.com

Servant Evangelism
http://www.servantevangelism.com

appendix b

Resources

The following is a list of resources that will assist you in the creation of your eMinistry. By no means is this a comprehensive list, but it's enough to get you started.

Books

Check with your local bookstore for price and availability. Most of these titles can be purchased for less than forty dollars.

Learning the Web

The Internet for Dummies by John R. Levine
Internet in a Nutshell by Valerie Quercia
Sams Teach Yourself HTML in 21 Days by Laura Lemay

eMinistry

AquaChurch: Essential Leadership Arts for Piloting Your Church in Today's Fluid Culture by Leonard Ira Sweet
eMinistry: Connecting with the Net Generation by Andrew Careaga
E-Vangelism: Sharing the Gospel in Cyberspace by Andrew Careaga
Handbook for Multi-Sensory Worship by Kim Miller
The Internet Church by Walter P. Wilson
Out on the Edge: A Wake-Up Call for Church Leaders on the Edge of the Media Reformation by Michael Slaughter

Post-Modern Pilgrims: First-Century Passion for the Twenty-first-Century Church by Leonard Ira Sweet

The Spectacle of Worship in a Wired World: Electronic Culture and the Gathered People of God by Tex Sample

The Wired Church: Making Media Ministry by Len Wilson

Web Design

The Art and Science of Web Design by Jeffrey Veen

Creating Killer Web Sites by David Siegel

Designing Web Graphics.3 by Lynda Weinman

Designing Web Usability by Jakob Nielsen

Don't Make Me Think! A Common Sense Approach to Web Usability by Steve Krug

The Geek's Guide to Internet Business Success by Bob Schmidt

Web Design in a Nutshell: A Desktop Quick Reference by Jennifer Niederst

Web Pages That Suck: Learn Good Design by Looking at Bad Design by Vincent Flanders and Michael Willis

Internet Service Providers (ISPs)

Earthlink (Cost: $21.95–$49.95 per month)
http://www.earthlink.com

MSN (Cost: $21.95–$39.95 per month)
www.msn.com

NetZero (Cost: Free–$9.95 per month)
http://www.netzero.com

Web Design Resources

Digital Dream Design (Cost: Variable)
Digital Dream is a professional design studio that specializes in Web

design and development. With more than seven years of experience, their team of professionals will help your eMinistry every step of the way.
http://www.digitaldreamdesign.com

Earthlink (Cost: $19.95–$34.95 per month)
An Internet services company that provides Click-n-Build, a publishing system for those who want a simple Web site without professional help.
http://www.earthlink.com

GospelCom (Cost: Free)
The most popular Christian Web site in the world, GospelCom is a collection of more than three hundred online ministries. Several feature resources, content, and freebies for eMinistry Web masters.
http://www.gospelcom.net

VeriSign (Cost: $19.95–$34.95 per month)
An Internet services company that features many different Web site packages and options, including point-and-click Web-site creation.
http://www.verisign.com

Other Resources

All of the following sites are free.

Finding Web Talent

FreeAgent.com
A site devoted to helping talent and employers find each other.
http://www.freeagent.com/

Guru.com
A site that matches companies with freelance Web design
   professionals.
http://www.guru.com/

Learning the Web

Builder.com
A comprehensive resource for learning how to build a Web site.
http://www.builder.com

eFuse.com
The friendly place to learn how to build a Web site.
http://www.efuse.com/

Hartford Institution for Religious Research
Links and instructive notes on how to plan and design church sites.
http://hirr.hartsem.edu/cong/cong.html

Lynda.com
Helps Web developers and designers understand how to use tools
   and design to enhance online communication.
http://www.lynda.com/

Web Evangelism Guide
The finest and most comprehensive Web site on Internet
   evangelism.
http://www.Web-evangelism.com

WebMonkey
A complete resource for Web developers.
http://hotwired.lycos.com/webmonkey

Endnotes

Introduction

1. Rick Warren, "Will the Next Generation Church Be on the Internet?" Ministry Tool Box, online: http://www.pastors.com, 23 July 2001, 1.

Chapter 1: The State of the Church

1. Win Arn, *The Pastor's Manual for Effective Ministry* (Monrovia, Calif.: Church Growth, 1988), 41.
2. Ibid., 43.
3. Carl S. Dudley and David A. Roozen, *Faith Communities Today: A Report on Religion in the United States Today,* March 2001, 10.
4. Randy Frazee with Lyle E. Schaller, *The Comeback Congregation* (Nashville: Abingdon, 1995), 11.
5. Benton Johnson, Dean R. Hoge, and Donald A. Luidens, "Mainline Churches: The Real Reason for Decline," *First Things* (March 1993), 13.
6. Constant H. Jacquet Jr., ed., *Yearbook of Canadian and American Churches, 1988* (Nashville: Abingdon, 1989), 261; cf. Eileen W. Lindner, ed., *Yearbook of American and Canadian Churches, 2001,* 347, 350, 355, 357. I have rounded these figures.
7. Scott Thumma, "Megachurches Cluster in Bible Belt, Study Shows," *Faith Communities Today* (FACT), The Hartford Institute for Religion Research, 6 December 2001, 1.

8. C. Peter Wagner, *Church Planting for a Greater Harvest* (Ventura, Calif.: Regal, 1990), 12, 14, 16.

9. Jackson W. Carroll, Douglas W. Johnson, and Martin E. Marty, *Religion in America: 1950 to the Present* (San Francisco: Harper & Row, 1979), 16.

10. Ibid.

11. Dean M. Kelley, *Why Conservative Churches Are Growing: A Study in the Sociology of Religion* (New York, N.Y.: Harper & Row, 1972).

12. Tom W. Smith, "Are Conservative Churches Growing?" online: http://www.icpsr.umich.edu, January 1991. Note that Smith uses the terms *conservative* and *fundamentalist* interchangeably.

13. Jacquet, *Yearbook of Canadian and American Churches, 1988,* 261; cf. Lindner, *Yearbook of American and Canadian Churches, 2001,* 353.

14. "Missions Memo," *Missions USA* 59, no. 4 (July–August 1988): 2.

15. Linda Lawson, "SBC '98 Stats Reveal First Drop since 1926," *Facts and Trends,* LifeWay Christian Resources, 3.

16. George Barna, "Church Attendance," Barna Research, online: http://www.barna.org, 3 December 2001. These figures were updated with information from an article titled "Worship Attendance Falls to Pre-Sept. 11 Levels," *Dallas Morning News,* 1 December 2001, 5G.

17. "Gallup Poll Topics: A–Z," The Gallup Organization, online: http://www.gallup.com, 13 December 2001.

18. Ibid.

19. Thomas C. Reeves, *The Empty Church* (New York: Simon & Schuster, 1996), 51.

20. "U.S. Attendance at Services Is Down in Poll," *Dallas Morning News,* 28 May 1994, 43A.

21. Cathy L. Grossman and Anthony DeBarros, "Still One Nation Under God," *USA Today,* 24 December 2001, 2D.

22. C. Kirk Hadaway, Penny L. Marler, and Mark Chaves, "What the Polls Don't Show: A Closer Look at U.S. Church Attendance," *American Sociological Review,* December 1993.

23. Christine Wicke, "Church Approves Land Deal," *Dallas Morning News,* 14 August 1995, 16A.
24. Frazee with Schaller, *The Comeback Congregation,* 39.
25. C. Kirk Hadaway and P. L. Marler, "Did You Really Go to Church This Week? Behind the Poll Data," *Religion Online,* online: http://www.religion-online.org, 10 December 2001, 3.
26. Ibid.
27. Ibid., 4.
28. Ibid., 7.
29. George Barna, "Church Attendance," *Barna Research,* online: http://www.barna.org, 15 October 1999.
30. Reeves, *The Empty Church,* 61.
31. "Latter Day Struggles," *U.S. News and World Report,* 28 September 1992, 73.
32. Jacquet, *Yearbook of Canadian and American Churches, 1988,* 262; cf. Lindner, *Yearbook of American and Canadian Churches, 2001,* 348, 352
33. *Dallas Morning News,* 16 February 2002, 1G.
34. Jacquet, *Yearbook of Canadian and American Churches, 1988,* 262; cf. Lindner, *Yearbook of American and Canadian Churches, 2001,* 348, 352.
35. "Muslim Mosques Growing at a Rapid Pace in the US," Hartford Seminary, online: http://fact.hartsem.edu., 1.
36. Ibid., 2.
37. Marcy E. Mullins, "A Measure of Faith," *USA Today,* 24 December 2001, 4D.
38. Thom S. Rainer, "Shattering Myths About the Unchurched," *Southern Baptist Journal of Theology* 5, no. 1 (spring 2001): 47.

Chapter 2: The Buck Stops Here!

1. Carl S. Dudley and David A. Roozen, *Faith Communities Today: A Report on Religion in the United States Today,* March 2001, 10.
2. "Study: One in Four U.S. Net Users Get Religion," CNN, online: http://www.cnn.com., 23 December 2001.

3. George Gallup Jr. and Jim Castelli, *The People's Religion: American Faith in the '90s* (New York: Macmillan, 1989), 132–39; The Princeton Religion Research Center, *The Unchurched American: 10 Years Later* (Princeton, N.J.: Princeton Religion Research Center, 1988), 2, 7.
4. Robert Bezilla, ed., *Religion in America: 1992–1993* (Princeton, N.J.: Princeton Religion Research Center, 1993), 44, 57, 62; "Religion Index Hits Ten-Year High," *Emerging Trends*, March 1996, 1–2.
5. Ibid., 45.
6. Wade Clark Roof and William McKinney, *American Mainline Religion: Its Changing Shape and Future* (New Brunswick, N.J.: Rutgers University Press, 1987), 44, 56.
7. Ibid.
8. Donald E. Messer, "Reinventing the Church," *Religion on Line*, online: www.religion-online.org, 12 December 2001, 1.
9. Ibid. Messer quotes a Eutychus column from *Christianity Today*.
10. William Easum, *Dancing with Dinosaurs: Ministry in a Hostile and Hurting World* (Nashville: Abingdon, 1993), 15.
11. Ibid.
12. "The Year's Most Intriguing Findings: From Barna Research Studies," *Barna Research*, online: http://www.barna.org, 17 December 2001, 2.
13. "Worship Attendance Falls to Pre-Sept. 11 Levels," *Dallas Morning News*, 1 December 2001, 5G.
14. Ibid.
15. "How America's Faith Has Changed Since 9-11," *Barna Research Online*, online: http://www.barna.org, 26 November 2001, 1.
16. "Gallup Poll Topics: A–Z," The Gallup Organization, online: http://www.gallup.com, 13 December 2001, 1.
17. Ibid.
18. "How America's Faith Has Changed," 4.
19. Thom S. Rainer, "Shattering Myths About the Unchurched," *Southern Baptist Journal of Theology* 5, no. 1 (spring 2001): 47.

20. Ibid.
21. "The Year's Most Intriguing Findings: From Barna Research Studies," 3.
22. Ibid.
23. Ibid., 2.

Chapter 3: Reaching New Generations

1. William Strauss and Neil Howe, *The Fourth Turning: An American Prophecy* (New York: Broadway Books, 1997), 16–17.
2. Ibid. For the sake of simplicity, I have merged two separate generations into one. I will use Strauss and Howe's generational markers to be consistent.
3. "Profile of General Demographic Characteristics for the United States: 2000," U.S. Census Bureau, online: http://www.census.gov., Table DP-1.
4. I (Aubrey) find it troubling that some Christian leaders will go to such extremes to discredit another ministry.
5. "Profile of General Demographic Characteristics for the United States: 2000," U.S. Census Bureau, Table DP-1.
6. Eric Reed, "Ministering with My Own Generation," *Leadership Journal,* fall 2000, 49.
7. "Church Attendance," Barna Research, online: http://www.barna.org, 15 October 1999, 46.
8. Ibid.
9. As with the other generations, different people view the beginning dates and ending dates differently for this generation. Thom Rainer follows the lead of *American Demographics* and sets the dates from 1977 to 1994. Thom S. Rainer, *The Bridger Generation* (Nashville: Broadman & Holman, 1997). However, I've followed the lead of generational historians Neil Howe and William Strauss, *Generations: The History of America's Future, 1854 to 2069* (New York: Morrow, 1991), who set it from 1982 to 2000.
10. Rainer, *Bridger Generation.*

11. Susan Mitchell, "The Next Baby Boom," *American Demographics* 17, no. 10 (October 1995): 25.
12. Jon Walker, "Internet Plays a Major Role in the Lives of U.S. Teens," Pastors.com, online: http://www.pastors.com, 27 September 2001.
13. "Church Attendance," Barna Research, online: http://www.barna.org, 15 October 1999.
14. "New Barna Book Provides Insight into Real Teens," Barna Research, online: http://www.barna.org, 8 October 2001, 3.
15. Thom S. Rainer, "Shattering Myths About the Unchurched," *Southern Baptist Journal of Theology* 5, no. 1 (spring 2001): 46–47.
16. Rainer, *Bridger Generation*, 13.
17. Ibid.

Chapter 4: Developing a Theology of Change

1. Michael E. Gerber, *The E-Myth* (New York: Harper Business, 1986), 156.
2. George Barna, *The Second Coming of the Church* (Nashville: Word, 1998), 8.
3. Mike Regele, *Death of the Church* (Grand Rapids: Zondervan, 1995), 204.
4. Barna, *Second Coming of the Church*, 8.
5. Francis Schaeffer, *The Church at the End of the Twentieth Century* (Wheaton, Ill.: Crossway, 1970), 68.

Chapter 5: Understanding Postmodernism

1. I don't use supernaturalism here in the sense that Christianity uses it. I'm using it in contrast to philosophical naturalism's idea that nothing exists outside the natural order of this material universe, that this material universe is the sum total of reality, whereas postmodernism believes that something does exist beyond the material universe; hence, a spiritual dimension exists in addition to the material dimension.

2. Paul Johnson, *Modern Times: The World from the Twenties to the Nineties* (New York: HarperCollins, 1991), 1–4.

3. Sally Morgenthaler, "Is Post-modernism Passe?" *Rev. Magazine,* September–October 2001, 70.

4. Marshall Shelley and Eric Reed, "Warrior, Chief, Medicine Man," *Leadership,* fall 2000, 54.

5. Lee Rainie, "CyberFaith: How Americans Pursue Religion Online," Pew Internet & American Life Project, online: http://www.pewinternet.org/, 23 December 2001, 2.

Chapter 6: The Importance of the Internet

1. "More Americans Are Seeking Net-based Faith Experiences," Barna Research Online, online: http://www.barna.org, 21 May 2001, 1.

2. Esther Dyson, "A Map of the Network Society," *New Perspective Quarterly,* spring 1997, 25.

3. Jeffrey I. Cole, "Surveying the Digital Future," *The UCLA Internet Report 2001,* online: http://www.ccp.ucla.edu, 3 December 2001, 5, 90.

4. Steven Levy, "Random Access," *Newsweek,* 7 July 1997.

5. "How Many Online?" *NUA Internet Surveys,* online: http://www.nua.ie, September 2002.

6. Jeffrey I. Cole, "Surveying the Digital Future," *The UCLA Internet Report 2003,* online: http://www.ccp.ucla.edu, February 2003.

7. Jeffrey I. Cole, "Surveying the Digital Future," *The UCLA Internet Report 2000,* online: http://www.ccp.ucla.edu, 17 November 2000, 4–5.

8. "Teens Prefer Internet to Telephone," *NUA Internet Surveys,* Online: http://www.nua.org, January 2002.

9. Michael Pastore, "Internet Use Continues to Pervade U.S. Life," *CyberAtlas,* online: http://cyberatlas.internet.com, 30 May 2001.

10. Cole, "Surveying the Digital Future," *UCLA Internet Report 2001,* 24.

11. Cole, "Surveying the Digital Future," *UCLA Internet Report 2003*, 59.
12. Ibid., 62.
13. Ibid., 78.
14. Elena Larsen, "CyberFaith: How Americans Pursue Religion Online," Pew Internet and American Life Project, online: http://www.pewinternet.org, December 2001, 1.
15. "Christians Embrace Technology," *Barna Research Online*, online: http://www.barna.org, June 2000.
16. Jonathan Gardner and Andrew Oswald, *Internet Use: The Digital Divide*, online: http://www.oswald.co.uk, November 2001, 8.
17. Larsen, "CyberFaith: How Americans Pursue Religion Online," 21.
18. Andrew Careaga, "Embracing the Cyberchurch," online: http://www.next-wave.org, December 1999.
19. Elena Larsen, "Wired Churches; Wired Temples," Pew Internet and American Life Project, online: http://www.pewinternet.org, December 2000, 2–3.

Chapter 7: Understanding the Internet

1. By putting it as simply as we have we run the risk of downplaying the awesome potential and far-reaching capabilities of the Net. Keep in mind that the Net is a much deeper and more complex system than any single definition can convey or than even several large books can cover. But, to use the Internet for Christ, we don't need to know all the ins and outs; it is enough just to be able to grasp what the Internet is, who is using it, and how it can be used for ministry.
2. J. C. R. Licklider and Robert Taylor, "The Computer as a Communication Device," *Science and Technology*, April 1968, 22.
3. "How Many Online?" *NUA Internet Surveys*, online: http://www.nua.ie, August 2001.
4. Michael Pastore, "Internet Use Continues to Pervade U.S. Life," *CyberAtlas*, online: http://cyberatlas.internet.com, 30 May 2001.
5. Jeffrey I. Cole, "Surveying the Digital Future," *The UCLA*

Internet Report 2003, online: http://www.ccp.ucla.edu, February 2003, 21.

6. Pastore, "Internet Use Continues to Pervade U.S. Life."
7. Andrew Careaga, "How the Internet Affects the Faith and Relationships of Christian Teenagers," online: http://www.e-vangelism.com/teens.htm, September 1999.
8. Don Tapscott, *Growing Up Digital: The Rise of the Net Generation* (New York: McGraw-Hill, 1999).
9. Cole, "Surveying the Digital Future," *The UCLA Internet Report 2003,* 18.
10. Amanda Lenhart, Lee Rainie, and Oliver Lewis, "Teenage Life Online," Pew Internet and American Life Project, online: http://www.pewinternet.org, June 2001, 3.
11. Cole, "Surveying the Digital Future," *The UCLA Internet Report 2003,* 18.
12. Elena Larsen, "CyberFaith: How Americans Pursue Religion Online," Pew Internet and American Life Project, online: http://www.pewinternet.org, December 2001, 2.
13. Ibid., 2
14. "Web Statistics," Web Characterization Project, online: http://wcp.oclc.org, 2002.
15. Larsen, "CyberFaith: How Americans Pursue Religion Online," 2.

Chapter 8: Putting the Internet to Work for Christ

1. John P. Martin, "Churches Use Net to Reach the Faithful," *Washington Post,* online: http://www.washingtonpost.com/wp-srv/local/daily/april99/religionweb10.htm, 10 April 1999.
2. "More Americans Are Seeking Net-Based Faith Experiences," Barna Research Online, online: http://www.barna.org, May 2001.
3. Martin, "Churches Use Net to Reach the Faithful."
4. Elena Larsen, "CyberFaith: How Americans Pursue Religion Online," Pew Internet and American Life Project, online: http://www.pewinternet.org, December 2001, 21.
5. Ibid.

6.   Arne H. Fjeldstad, "Communicating the Gospel on the Internet," online: http://www.geocities.com/ResearchTriangle/ 1541/survey1.html, June 2003.

7.   Andrew Careaga, "How the Internet Affects the Faith and Relationships of Christian Teenagers," online: http://www.e-vangelism.com/teens.htm, September 1999.

8.   "More Americans Are Seeking Net-Based Faith Experiences."

9.   Ibid.

10. John Dart, "Connected Congregations," Hartford Institute for Religious Research, online: http://hirr.hartsem.edu/research/ research_religion_web_articles1.html, 2001.

11. Ken Bedell, "Dispatches from the Electronic Frontier," online: http://www.religion-research.org/Dispatches.htm, May 1998.

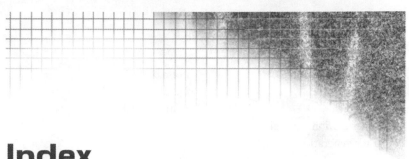

Index

"seeker" service, 50–51
Smith, Jane I., 26
Smith, Tom, 16
Solomon, 67
Southern Baptist Convention, 16–17, 38–39, 47, 143–44
Southern Baptist Theological Seminary, 38
Strauss, William, 45
Sunday, religious observance of, 32–33
supernatural, interest in, 77, 79, 162

T
Tapscott, Don, 115
technology, 95–148; church and, 70, 90–91; information, 9, 59, 95–99, 103–8, 109–15, 121–24; recent generations and, 56. *See also* eMinistry.
teenagers, 8, 12, 33, 56–57, 114, 121, 134–35
television, 98, 104
theism, 78–79
theology of change, 5, 44, 59, 61–63, 65, 67, 69, 71,73, 75
theooze.com, 99–103, 133
thirteenth generation, 52. *See also* generational demographics.
Thumma, Scott, 16, 144
tolerance, 80, 83–84
Tomlinson, Ray, 111
twentieth century, 14, 32, 47, 57, 60, 80
twenty-first century, 26–27, 57, 81, 87; church planting, 51–52,

63–64, 67, 147–48; technological culture, 9, 70, 90–91, 114–15, 118; traditional church in, 13–14, 29–40, 44

U
U.S. News and World Report, 25
UCLA, 97–98, 104, 121
"unchurched" population, 23–24, 30–31, 38, 50–51, 56, 61, 85. *See also* "churched" population.
United Methodist Church, 15, 132
United States Postal Service, 98, 111
URL, 143
USA Today, 21

V
value evangelism, 38, 40
VeriSign, 144
Vietnam, 49

W
Warren, Rick, 8, 70
Washunk Baptist Church, 143–44
Waters, Dooney, 56
Web design, 144, 154–55. *See also* World Wide Web.
webcasts, 131
webmaster, 99, 115, 140
Western worldviews, 79
What Congregations Do With Their Websites survey, 131
White House Web, 125

White House, 125–26
Wicca, 26
Willow Creek Community
    Church, 50–51, 54, 70, 131, 150
World War I, 46
World War II, 14–15, 21, 25, 30,
    46, 49
World Wide Web, importance of,
    103–8, 121, 130–32;
    "information superhighway,"
    123–27; Internet and, 110–12;
    sites on, 97, 100, 115–20, 131,
    132–43, 144, 149–52; use of,
    97–98, 121–23. *See also* e-mail;
    eMinistry; Internet.
worldview, 44, 78–80, 83
worship; attendance, 17, 32–33;
    format/style, 47–48, 50–51, 54,
    65–70, 71, 87–88; freedom, 30;
    online, 116, 131, 136, 139

X
X, generation, 52, 99

Y
Y, generation, 55
Yale Web Style Guide, 146
Yearbook of American and
    Canadian Churches, 25

digitaldreamdesign

Are you ready to begin building your eMinistry?

Digital Dream Design can provide you with the Web site development services you need. We are Web professionals that specialize in incorporating striking visual design with strong marketing strategies and groundbreaking development. We work closely with both churches and businesses to deliver unique solutions that prevent them from getting lost on the Web. The result? Success.

For more information, contact Michael Malphurs at:

mike@digitaldreamdesign.com

or

visit our Web site at:

www.digitaldreamdesign.com